GREYSTONE'S

Creative Hands

EDITOR

Beverley Hilton

 GREYSTONE PRESS/NEW YORK · TORONTO · LONDON

Volume 19

Contents

QUICK MAKE
Pull-on hat

A quick little pull-on hat to crochet. Make it in any color to wear with your favorite coat and pin on a bright brooch just for fun.

Size

To fit average adult head

Gauge

About 1 loop to 1 in over patt worked on No.G hook and using yarn double.

Materials

Sports Yarn
2 ounces
One No. G (4.50 mm) crochet hook

Hat

Using No.G hook and yarn double throughout, ch4. Join with ss into first ch to form a circle.

1st round *Ch4, 1sc into circle, rep from * 3 times more.

2nd round * Ch4, 1sc into loop, ch4, 1sc into next sc, rep from * 3 times more.

3rd round Ss to center of first loop of last round, *ch4, 1sc into next loop, rep from * 6 times more, ch4, 1sc into ss.

4th round *Ch4, 1sc into loop, ch4, 1sc into next sc, rep from * 7 times more.

5th round Ss to center of first loop of last round, *ch4, 1sc into next loop, rep from * 14 times more, ch4, 1sc into ss.

Rep 5th round 3 times more.

9th round Ss to center of first loop of last round, *ch4, 1sc into same loop (ch4, 1sc into next loop) 4 times, rep from * 3 times more, 1sc into ss. 20 loops.

10th round Ss to center of first loop of last round, *ch4,

1sc into next loop, rep from * 18 times more, ch4, 1sc into ss:

Rep 10th round 10 times more.

21st round *2sc into next loop, 1sc into next sc, rep from * to end of round, ending with ss into first sc.

22nd round Ch1, *sc into back of next sc, rep from * to end of round, ending with ss into first ch.

Rep 22nd round 5 times more. Fasten off.

Finishing

Run in all ends.
Press lightly under a damp cloth using a warm iron.

▼ *Enlarged detail of the simple stitch used for the pull-on hat*

1981

The inside-out coat

This lightweight, hooded coat in two-color stripes is reverse stockinette stitch. Wear it as a coat, teamed with pants, or as a coat-dress.

Sizes

Directions are for 34in bust and 36in hips.
The figures in brackets [ ] refer to 36 and 38in bust and 38 and 40in hips respectively.
Length to shoulder, 40[40½:41]in
Sleeve seam, 17in

Gauge

7 sts and 9 rows to 1in over reversed st st worked on No. 4 needles.

Materials

3-ply fingering yarn
12 [13:15] 1 oz. balls main color, A, pink
9 [11:12] balls contrasting color B, white
One pair No. 3 needles (or Canadian No. 10)
One pair No. 4 needles (or Canadian No. 9)
6 buttons

Back

Using No.4 needles and A, cast on 150[156:162] sts.
Commence striped patt, using separate balls of A and B where necessary.
Using A and beg with a P row, work 6 rows reversed st st, then work (1 row B, 1 row A) twice, then 6 rows B. These 16 rows form patt and are rep throughout.
Continue in patt until work measures 6in from beg, ending with a K row.

Shape sides

Dec one st at each end of next and every following 8th row until 120[126:132] sts rem, then at each end of every following 6th row until 110[116:122] sts rem.
Continue without shaping until work measures 24½in from beg, ending with a K row.
Inc onc st at each end of next and every following 6th row until there are 126[132:138] sts.
Continue without shaping until work measures 34in from beg or desired length to underarm, allowing 1in for hem and ending with a K row.

Shape armholes

Bind off 4 sts at beg of next 2 rows; then 2 sts at beg of next 4 rows.
Dec one st at each end every other row 4[5:6] times. 102[106:110] sts.
Continue without shaping until armholes measure 7[7½:8]in from beg, ending with a K row.

Shape shoulders

Bind off 8 sts at beg of next 6 rows, then 8[9:10] sts at beg of next 2 rows.
Bind off rem 38[40:42] sts.

Right front

Using No.4 needles and A, cast on 75[79:83] sts.
Work in patt as given for Back until work measures 6in from beg, ending with a K row.

Shape side

Dec one st at end of next and every following 8th row until 60[64:68] sts rem, then at end of every following 6th row until 55[59:63] sts rem.
Continue without shaping until work measures 24½in from beg, ending with a K row.
Inc one st at end of next and every following 6th row until there are 63[67:71] sts.
Continue without shaping until work measures same as Back to underarm, ending with a P row.

Shape armhole

At armhole edge, bind off 4 sts; then 2 sts every other row twice.
Dec one st at armhole edge every other row 4[5:6] times. 51[54:57] sts.
Continue without shaping until armhole measures 5¾[6¼:6¾]in from beg, ending with a K row.

Shape neck

At neck edge, bind off 10[12:14] sts once and 3 sts every other row 3 times. 32[33:34] sts.
Continue without shaping until armhole measures same as Back to shoulder, ending with a P row.

Shape shoulder

At armhole edge, bind off 8 sts every other row 3 times and 8[9:10] sts once.

Left front

Work as given for Right front, reversing all shaping.

Sleeves

Using No.4 needles and A, cast on 58[61:64] sts.
Work in patt as given for Back for 2½in.
Continue in patt, inc one st at each end of next and every following 8th row until there are 88[91:94] sts.
Continue without shaping until sleeve measures 18in from beg or desired length to underarm, allowing 1in for hem and ending with a K row and same patt as for Back.

Shape cap

Bind off 4 sts at beg of next 2 rows and 2 sts at beg of next 4 rows.
Dec one st at each end of next and following 9[10:11] alt rows. 52[53:54] sts.
Bind off 2 sts at beg of next 8 rows, 3 sts at beg of next 4 rows and 4 sts at beg of next 2 rows. Bing off rem 16[17:18] sts.

Hood

Using No.4 needles and A cast on 136 sts.
Work in patt as given for Back for 13in, ending with a K row.
Bind off loosely or leave sts to weave tog later.

Border

Mark positions for 6 buttonholes on Right front edge, first to come just below neck edge with 5 more evenly spaced 6in apart.
Join shoulder seams. Fold Hood in half and join top edge, then sew cast-on edge to neck edge.
Using No.3 needles and A, cast on 21 sts.
1st row K1, *ytf, sl 1P, ytb, K1, rep from * to end.
2nd row Ytf, sl 1P, *ytb, K1, ytf, sl 1P, rep from * to end.
Rep these 2 rows until border is level with first buttonhole position, allowing 1in for hem, ending with a 2nd row.
Next row (buttonhole row) Patt 7 sts, bind off 7 sts, patt to end.
Next row Patt 7 sts, cast on 7 sts over bound-off sts, patt to end.
Continue in patt, working 5 more buttonholes as markers are reached, until border fits around front edges, ending with a 1st row.
Bind off K2 tog across the row.

Finishing

Press each piece under a damp cloth with a warm iron. Sew in sleeves. Join side and sleeve seams.
Turn up 1in hem at lower edge and sleeve edges and slip stitch in place.
Sew on border. Press all seams. Sew on buttons.

1983

1984

Two-piece for tinies

The top of this suit has delicate embroidered flower motifs. Solid matching pants complete the outfit.

Size

Directions are for 20/22in chest.
Pullover. Length to shoulder, 12½in.
Sleeve seam, 9in.
Pants. Length at side, 7½in.

Gauge
7 sts and 9 rows to 1in over st st worked on No. 3 needles

Materials

3-ply fingering yarn pale pink, 5 ounces
One pair No. 2 needles (or Canadian No. 11)
One pair No. 3 needles (or Canadian No. 10)
One No. E (3.50 mm) crochet hook
3 buttons
Waist-length elastic
Small lengths of embroidery silks in shell pink, rose pink, green and white

Pullover back

Using No.3 needles, cast on 77 sts.
Beg with a P row, work 65 rows st st.

Shape armholes

Bind off 3 sts at beg of next 2 rows and 2 sts at beg of next 2 rows.
Dec one st at each end every other row 3 times.
Continue without shaping until 46 rows have been worked from beg of armhole shaping.

Shape neck and shoulders

Next row K22, bind off 17 sts, K to end.
Complete this side first.
At armhole edge, bind off 4 sts every other row 3 times, *at the same time* bind off at neck edge on every other row 3 sts once, 2 sts once and one st once.
Bind off rem 4 sts.
With WS facing, attach yarn to rem sts and complete to correspond to first side, reversing shapings.

Pullover front

Using No.3 needles, cast on 77 sts.
P 1 row.
Commence patt.
1st row K2, (sl 1, K1, psso, ytf) 36 times, K3.
2nd row P.
3rd row K2, (sl 1, K1, psso, ytf, K8) 7 times, sl 1, K1, psso, ytf, K3.
Rep 2nd and 3rd rows 5 times more, then 2nd row once.
15th row As 1st.
16th row P.
17th row K12, (sl 1, K1, psso, ytf, K8) 5 times, sl 1, K1, psso, ytf, K13.
Rep 16th and 17th rows 5 times more, then 16th row once.
29th row K12, (sl 1, K1, psso, ytf) 26 times, K13.
30th row P.
31st row K22, (sl 1, K1, psso, ytf, K8) 3 times, sl 1, K1, psso, ytf, K23.
Rep 30th and 31st rows 5 times more, then 30th row once.
43rd row K22, (sl 1, K1, psso, ytf) 16 times, K23.
44th row P.
45th row K32, sl 1, K1, psso, ytf, K8, sl 1, K1, psso, ytf, K33.
Rep 44th and 45th rows 5 times more, then 44th row once.
57th row K32, (sl 1, K1, psso, ytf) 6 times, K33.
Beg with a P row, work 7 rows st st.

Shape armholes

Work as given for Back, then continue without shaping until 34 rows have been worked from beg of armhole shaping.

Shape neck

Next row K24, bind off 13 sts, K to end.
Complete this side first.
P 1 row.
Bind off at neck edge on every other row 3 sts once, 2 sts once and one st 3 times. 16 sts.
Work 2 rows st st, working 47 in all from beg of armhole shaping.

Shape shoulder

Bind off at armhole edge every other row 4 sts 4 times.
With WS facing, attach yarn to rem sts and complete to correspond to first side, reversing shaping.

Sleeves

Using No.3 needles, cast on 44 sts.
Beg with a P row, continue in st st, inc one st at each end of every 6th row until there are 62 sts.
Continue without shaping until 79 rows have been worked from beg.

Shape cap

Bind off 3 sts at beg of next 2 rows and 2 sts at beg of next 4 rows.
Dec one st at each end every other row 8 times, ending with a P row.
Bind off 2 sts at beg of next 6 rows and 3 sts at beg of next 2 rows.
Bind off rem 14 sts.

Finishing

Press each piece lightly under a damp cloth with a cool iron.
Join right shoulder seam and left shoulder seam for ½in from armhole edge.
Sew in sleeves. Join side and sleeve seams.
Using No.E hook, work a row sc along each side of left shoulder opening, working 3 button loops on front shoulder.

Neck edging

Using No.E hook and with RS facing, work a row sc around neck edge. Turn.
Next row * Ch4, ss into first of these 4ch to form picot, 1sc into each of next 2 sts, skip one st, ss into next st, rep from * to end. Fasten off.
Work around lower edge and cuffs in same manner. Press seams. Sew on 3 buttons to left back shoulder.
Using embroidery silks, work a flower motif in every other square on front, as illustrated.

Pants

Using No.2 needles, cast on 71 sts and beg at front waist.
1st row K1, *P1, K1, rep from * to end.
2nd row P1, *K1, P1, rep from * to end.
Rep these 2 rows for 2in, ending with a 2nd row.
Change to No.3 needles.
Beg with a K row, work 34 rows st st.

Shape legs

Bind off 8 sts at beg of next 2 rows, 5 sts at beg of next 2 rows, 4 sts at beg of next 2 rows, 3 sts at beg of next 2 rows and 2 sts at beg of next 2 rows.
Dec one st each end every other row 4 times. 19 sts.
Work 11 rows st st without shaping, working 62 rows in all from beg of st st.
Cast on 2 sts at beg of next 26 rows.
Work 34 rows st st without shaping.

Shape back

Next 2 rows K to last 7 sts, turn, P to last 7 sts. Turn.
Next 2 rows K to last 14 sts, turn, P to last 14 sts. Turn.
Continue working 7 sts less in this manner on next 4 rows, then K across all sts.
P 1 row.
Change to No.2 needles.
Work 2in rib as given at beg.
Bind off loosely in rib.

Finishing

Press as given for Pullover.
Join side seams. Fold waist ribbing in half to WS and slip stitch in place. Thread elastic through waist.
Work crochet edging around each leg as given for Pullover. Press seams.

The glint of gold

This small but striking piece of metal thread embroidery is surprisingly versatile. It can be worked as an article of embroidered jewelery making a choker, belt buckle or a decorative ornament for a handbag or it can adorn the top of a small, very special box.

The effectiveness of the piece depends largely upon the careful choice of gold threads, beads, scraps of kid and gold purl to suit the design and the background fabric.

Basic materials for gold work

Metal thread embroidery must be worked on a hoop. It is essential that the

▲ A pendant worked in metal thread embroidery is teamed with a suede choker for a smart accessory

fabric is held taut, both to support the threads in smooth lines and to avoid puckering. An embroidery frame is recommended for large pieces of work, while a hoop is suitable for smaller pieces measuring up to about 12 inches square.

The range of metal embroidery threads includes synthetic types as well as pure gold and silver threads. It is important to consider which will tarnish and discolor slightly with exposure—synthetic threads will not—although this irregularity may heighten the interest and contrast of the work.

When selecting a material for metal thread work, choose one that is closely woven. Tweed, soft wool, home furnishing linen, pure silk and velvet are all suitable and are worth considering as effective background materials. Before starting gold work it is advisable to back the base fabric with a material of approximately the same weight. Linen, cotton or muslin are all suitable but backing material should always be pre-shrunk before use.

Making a pendant

The design made up as a circular pen-

dant and worn with a choker, as shown here, is mounted on two thicknesses of cardboard for strength. The embroidery is worked on a small piece of woolen fabric, the reverse side is covered with leather, and tiny beads are stitched along the joining seam. Two flat buckles with the prongs removed are tied together to form the mounting for the piece. The size and shape of the buckles can be varied at will, or a single buckle or metal ring substituted if the pendant is to be worn on a chain.

Quick change to a belt

The same piece of work adapts easily for use as a gleaming buckle or ornament on a belt of leather, cloth or suede, cut to the correct size as shown. The belt is made in two sections, laced at the back, and is fixed to the buckle without stitching or glueing as shown.

A gem of a box top

The design can be enlarged slightly to make an elaborate box top. Velvet or felt in rich, jewel-like colors would make a particularly suitable background fabric for the lid of a dainty trinket or button box.

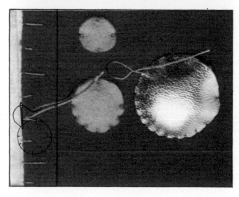

▲ *The same ornament can be easily adapted to wear with a belt*

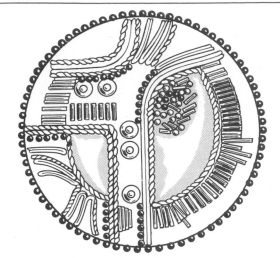

Tracing pattern of the design

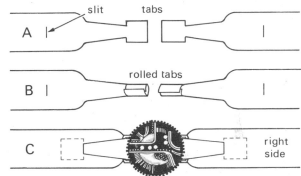

A simple method of attaching the embroidered buckle to the belt: (a) The belt is in two sections as shown. (b) Roll the tab at each end. (c) Push tab through the mounting and back through the slit in the belt to wrong side

Simple couching effects. The method of couching down metal threads, the needle angled to insure that the stitches lie closely together; double stitches worked at the beginning and end of a row and bricked couching; couching stitches evenly distributed; two ways of couching down flat braids using large couching stitches or small diagonal back stitches; flat braid couched down with tiny back stitches down the center of the braid; a method for couching down twisted metal thread, the stitches made at an angle to the twist and into the middle of the thread; a method of couching purl purl, small angled stitches being made between the twists of purl

Progressive stages of making a padded area. The smallest piece of felt is stitched down first and each larger layer is stitched over the smaller layer in turn, with the gold kid on top. Four stab-stitches are made around the edge of each piece, then the rest of the stitches are filled in

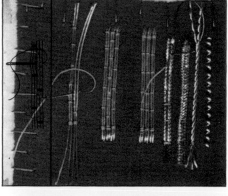

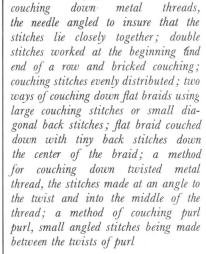

A few more ideas for using this attractive gold work design

A simple wild pansy purse worked in three stitches

NEEDLEPOINT FOLIO

Small gifts to make

Many people who might be tempted to try their hand at needlepoint are daunted by the large and intricate pieces of work they see in shops and magazines. Although these large pieces can provide inspiration, the inexperienced embroiderer needs en-

couragement in the form of smaller, simple pieces. These should be well designed and colorful enough to be fun to make and pleasing to give.

Any of the needlepoint articles shown here is simple enough to be worked by someone new to this form of embroidery – or might just as effectively be worked in more complex stitches by the experienced embroiderer.

A tiny wild pansy inspired the motif for the change purse in needlepoint and the glasses case is based on an abstract form of the same shape. The design for the purse has been kept very simple and all unnecessary detail omitted. The central motif is outlined with a felt-tipped pen and traced through onto the canvas. The natural colors of the flower are worked in three stitches: tent stitch for the outline of the design, small diagonal stitch for the flower and mosaic stitch for the background.

The flower shape has been further

simplified for the glasses case and the resulting design is more stylized. The central figures are worked in cross-stitch, and cushion stitch is used for the background. When the stitchery has been completed, block the canvas, then stretch over a piece of thin cardboard cut to the shape required, glueing the turnings to the reverse side. Glue a piece of felt cut to size to the reverse side for the lining of the glasses case.

The design can be repeated on the reverse side of the case, or the reverse side can be worked in cushion stitch in just one toning color. After stitching the two sides of the glasses case together, cover the join with velvet ribbon or cord. Alternatively, work an edge stitch around each piece of canvas, then stitch the two sides together. The tiny lighter case is a simple rectangular strip of canvas worked in a variation of bricking stitch (see stitch detail), folded in half and sewn up along the sides. An edge stitch finishes off the piece along the folded edges.

Making a pincushion

1. *Choose a simple motif or design for a square or rectangular pincushion and make a chart on graph paper before beginning to work. Each small square on the chart represents one stitch. A combination of stitches will provide a pleasing contrast in texture. For instance tent, Gobelin, straight and satin stitches are all smooth. Cross, rice and star stitches are semi-rough. Double cross, oblong and tufted stitches are very rough. Remember that strong texture is often most effective when used in small areas.*

2. *A monogram or single letter is easy to work out on a chart, and makes a particularly appealing pincushion. The letter or letters might be worked in tent stitch and the background in cushion stitch or alternating rows of tent stitch and long-legged cross stitch. Use tapestry yarns and work on single-weave canvas with 14 threads to the inch, using a No. 20 tapestry needle*

3. *After the design has been worked, block the canvas and trim off the excess, allowing ⅝ inch turnings. For the backing, cut a square or rectangle of velvet or other sturdy fabric to the size of the trimmed canvas. Baste the turnings to the wrong side to make a neat, accurate square or rectangle. Baste the canvas turnings to the back of the work and pin the velvet to the canvas, wrong sides together. Hem the velvet firmly into place, stitching into the outer row of needlepoint stitches. Leave half of one side open for stuffing. Bran, sheepswool and emery powder are all suitable materials for stuffing and should be packed in very tightly. Close the opening with pins and hem tightly when fully stuffed. Make neat by sewing cord all around the edge, covering the seam*

▼ *Rich colors and an elegant design for a glasses case*

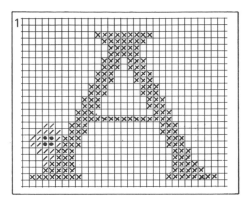
1

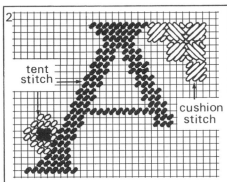
2

tent stitch

cushion stitch

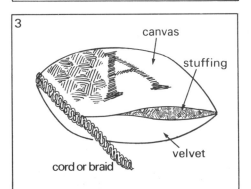
3

canvas

stuffing

velvet

cord or braid

▲ *A single stitch is used for this tiny lighter case*
▼ *A variation of bricking stitch: each stitch is worked over two threads*

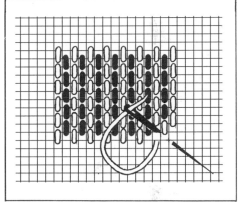

▼ *Other gift-giving ideas in needlepoint*

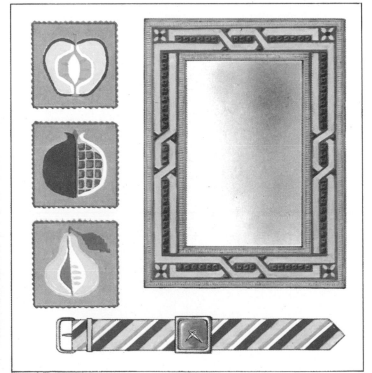

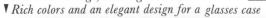

Make a grab bag

Knit or crochet one of these beautiful bags – they'll hold everything you could possibly wish, either as a handbag or as a work bag.

Crochet bag

Size

15½in wide at lower edge by 12in deep, excluding handles.

Gauge
5 sts and 5 rows to 1in worked on No.E hook

Materials

3-ply fingering yarn
2, 1 oz. skeins Black, A
2, 1 oz. skeins Snow White, B
2, 1 oz. skeins Beige, C
One No. E (3.50 mm) crochet hook
One pair wooden handles

Using No.E hook and A, ch67.

1st row 1sc into 2nd ch from hook, *1sc into next ch, rep from * to end. Turn. 66 sc.

Next row Ch2, *1sc into next sc, rep from * to end. Turn.

Rep last row 4 times more.

Next row Ss over first 4sc, ch2, *1sc into next sc, rep from * to within last 4sc. Turn. 58sc.

Next row Ch5, 1sc into 2nd ch from hook, 1sc into each of next 3ch, 1sc into each of next 58sc, ch5. Turn.

Next row 1sc into 2nd ch from hook, 1sc into each of next 3ch, 1sc into each of next 62sc. Turn. 66sc.

Next row Ch2, *1sc into next sc, rep from * to end. Turn.

Rep last row 4 times more. Fasten off A.

Continue in patt as follows.

1st row Attach C to first sc, ch3 to count as first dc, 1dc into each of next 5sc, 2dc into next sc, (1dc into each of next 6sc, 2dc into next sc) 3 times, 1sc into each of next 10sc, (2dc into next sc, 1dc into each of next 6sc) 4 times. Turn. Fasten off C. 74dc.

2nd row Attach A to first dc, *1sc into next dc, rep from * to end, 1sc into 3rd of 3ch.

Turn. Fasten off A.

3rd row Attach B to first sc, ch3 to count as first dc, 1dc into each of next 6sc, 2dc into next sc, (1dc into each of next 7sc, 2dc into next sc) 3 times, 1dc into each of next 10sc, (2dc into next sc, 1dc into each of next 7sc) 4 times. Turn. Fasten off B. 82dc.

4th row Attach C, ch2 to count as first sc, *1sc into next dc, rep from * to end, 1sc into 3rd of 3ch. Turn. Fasten off C.

5th row Attach B, ch3 to count as first dc, 1dc into each of next 7dc, 2dc into next sc, 1dc into each of next 8sc, 2dc into next sc, 1dc into each of next 46sc, (2dc into next sc, 1dc into each of next 8sc) twice. Turn. 86dc.

6th row Ch3 to count as first dc, 1dc into next dc, *work 1dc into each st as follows: 2A, 2B, 2C, 2B, rep from * to within last 4 sts, work 2C, 2B. Turn. Fasten off A and C.

7th row Using B, ch3, *1dc into next dc, rep from * to end, 1 dc into 3rd of 3ch. Turn. Fasten off B.

8th row Attach C, ch2, 1sc into each of next 8dc, 2sc into next dc, 1sc into each of next 9dc, 2sc into next dc, 1sc into each of next 46dc, (2sc into next dc, 1sc into each of next 9dc) twice. Turn. Fasten off C. 90sc.

9th row Attach B, ch3, *1dc into next dc, rep from * to end, 1dc into 2nd of 2ch. Turn. Fasten off B.

10th row Attach A and work 1 row sc. Turn. Fasten off A.

11th–13th rows Attach C and work 3 rows dc. Turn. Fasten off C.

14th row Attach A and work 1 row sc. Turn. Fasten off A.

15th row Attach B and work 1 row dc. Turn.

16th row Work 1 row sc as follows: 4A, 2B, *7A, 2B, rep from * 8 times more, 3B. Turn.

17th row Work 1 row dc as follows: 2B, 1A, *2B, 1A, 5B, 1A, rep from * 8 times more 2B, 1A, 3B. Turn.

18th row Work 1 row sc as follows: 4A, *2B, 1A, 2B, 4A, rep from * 8 times more, (2B, 1A) twice. Turn.

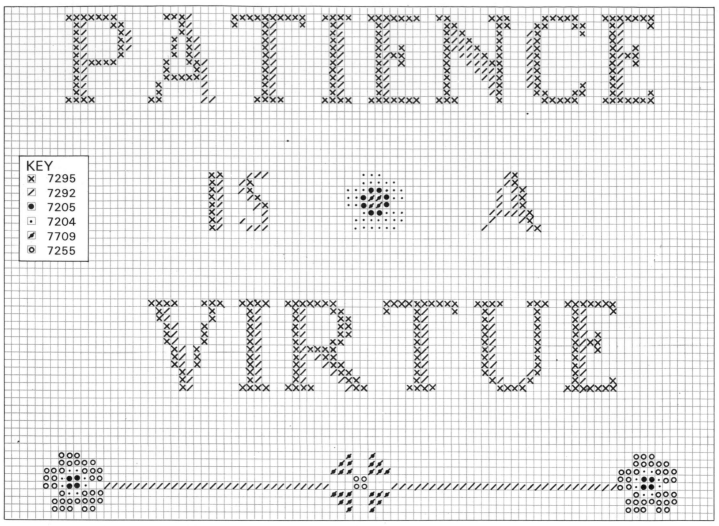

Chart for Duplicate stitch embroidery. Each square represents one stitch and lower border is repeated above

KEY
☒	7295
⧄	7292
⊙	7205
⊡	7204
◪	7709
⊚	7255

19th row Work 1 row dc as follows: 1A, *2B, 1A, 5B, 1A, rep from * 9 times more. Turn.

20th row Work 1 row sc as follows: *7A, 2B, rep from* to end. Turn.

21st row As 7th.

22nd row As 10th.

23rd–25th rows As 11th-13th.

26th row As 10th.

27th row As 7th.

28th row As 4th.

29th row As 7th.

30th row As 6th.

31st row As 7th.

32nd row As 4th.

33rd row As 7th.

34th row As 10th.

35th row As 4th.

36th row Attach A, ch3, leaving last loop of each on hook work 1dc into each of next 2dc, yrh and draw through all loops on hook – called dec 1 –, *1dc into next dc, rep from * to within last 3 sts, dec 1, 1dc into

3rd of 3ch.
Rep last row 4 times more.
Fasten off.

Work a second side in the same manner.

Finishing

Sew up side seams.
Make lining of stiffening fabric and fabric lining and insert into bag. Slip stitch lightly in place.
Turn top straight pieces through slot in handles and slip stitch in place.

Knitted bag

Size

17in wide at lower edge by 11in deep, excluding handles

Gauge

7 sts and 9 rows to 1in over st st worked on No. 3 needles

Materials

3-ply fingering yarn
4, 1 oz. skeins off-white
D.M.C. Tapestry
2 skeins of color No. 7295
1 skein each of colors
Nos. 7295, 7292, 7204, 7205, 7709 and 7255
One pair No. 3 needles
 (or Canadian No. 10)
One tapestry needle
One pair wooden handles

Using No. 3 needles, cast on 77 sts.
Beg with a K row, work 18 rows st st.
Inc twice at each end of next 4 rows. 93 sts.
Inc one st at each end every other row 4 times. 101 sts.

Next row P.

Inc one st at each end of next and following 5th row. 105 sts.
Inc one st at each end of every following 10th row until there are 117 sts.
Work without shaping for

16 rows more.

Next row (fold line) P.

Beg with a P row, work 16 rows st st.
Dec one st at each end of next and every following 10th row until 103 sts rem.
Dec one st at each end of the following 5th row. 101 sts.
Dec one st at each end every other row 4 times. 93 sts.
Dec 2 sts at each end of following 4 rows. 77 sts.
Work without shaping for 18 rows more. Bind off.

Duplicate stitch

Press work with a warm iron under a damp cloth.
Counting along the bound-off edge from left to right, mark the 39th st for center.
Counting down from this stitch, mark the 38th row with a colored thread.
Working into stitch to the left of marker and following the chart, begin with letter I of 'Patience'.

Slim-fit pants

Make these pants in a dramatic plaid fabric to team up with a sweater or blouse or jacket for a fashionable casual look. The pants are cut on classic lines with straight legs for style and easy movement.

Fabrics and notions

For the pants in all sizes you will need:

☐ $2\frac{3}{4}$ yards 36 inch wide fabric *or*,
☐ 2 yards 54 inch wide fabric

Note. Allow extra material for matching design on plaid fabrics. (Between $\frac{1}{4}$ and $\frac{1}{2}$ yard depending on size of plaid.)

☐ 8 inch zipper
☐ One $\frac{3}{4}$ inch button
☐ $\frac{1}{8}$ yard 36 inch wide interfacing
☐ 2 hook and eye fastenings
☐ Matching sewing thread
☐ Graph paper for patterns

The pattern

The pattern is given in size 25 inch, $26\frac{1}{2}$ inch, 28 inch or 30 inch waist measurement and to fit a $34\frac{1}{2}$ inch, 36 inch, 38 inch or 40 inch hip measurement. Make the back and front pants and waistband patterns from those on the graph.

The squares on the graph represent 1 inch squares. A seam allowance of $\frac{5}{8}$ inch has been allowed on all seams and $2\frac{5}{8}$ inches for the hem on the pants legs.

Cutting out

Lay out the pattern on the fabric as shown, matching the notches to the plaid of the fabric.

Making the pants

Darts

1. With right sides together, baste and stitch the front waist darts. Press the darts toward the center front.

2. With right sides together, baste and stitch the back waist darts. Press the darts toward the center back.

Seams

3. With right sides together, matching

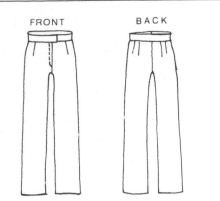

FRONT   BACK

notches, baste and stitch the inside leg seam and the side seam. Press the seams open.

Crotch

4. With right sides together, matching notches and inside leg seam, baste and stitch the crotch seam to small circle. Clip the curved edges and press the seam open.

5. Turn and baste the seam allowance of the right front to the wrong side and press. Place the zipper face down to the left front opening. Baste and stitch in place using the zipper foot on the machine.

6. Baste and stitch the right front to the zipper as shown. If desired, edge stitch the seam close to the zipper teeth on the left-hand side as shown.

7. Baste the interfacing to the wrong side of the waistband and catch stitch it down to the fold line.

8. With right sides together, matching notches, baste and stitch the waistband to the pants waist. Trim the interfacing close to stitching and trim and grade the seam. Press the seam up toward the waistband.

9. With right sides together, fold the waistband on the fold line and stitch the ends as shown. Clip the seam at center front to the stitching as shown. Trim and grade the seam and clip across the corners.

10. Turn the waistband to the inside basted edges. Baste and press. Turn under the seam allowance and hem to the stitching line.

11. Try on the pants and mark the hem. Baste around the folded edge. Trim the hem to an even width all around. Make neat the raw edge of the hem with hand overcasting or machine stitch. Sew the hem with invisible hemming stitch.

12. Work a hand- or machine-made buttonhole in the left front waistband in the position indicated on the pattern. Stitch the button on to the right front waistband on the under band. Stitch on the hooks and eyes at the waistband opening as shown.

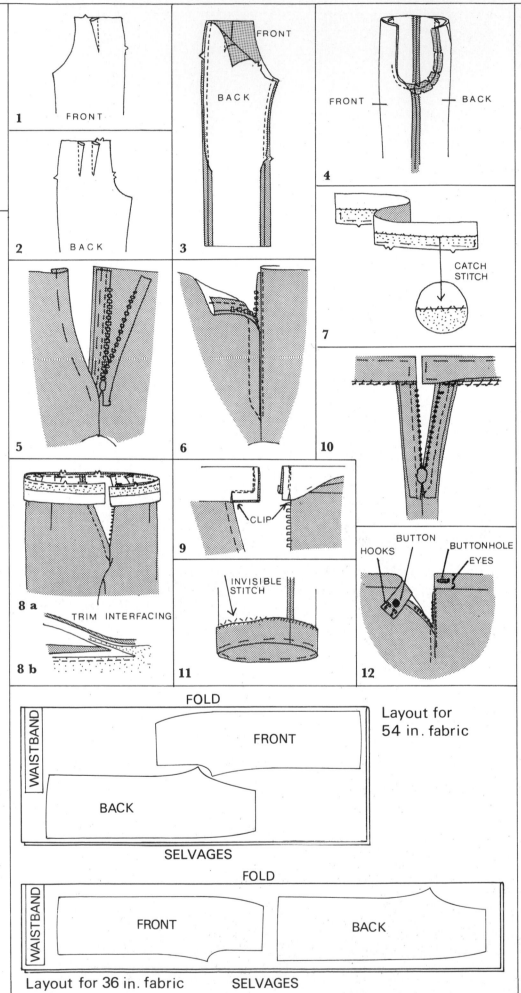

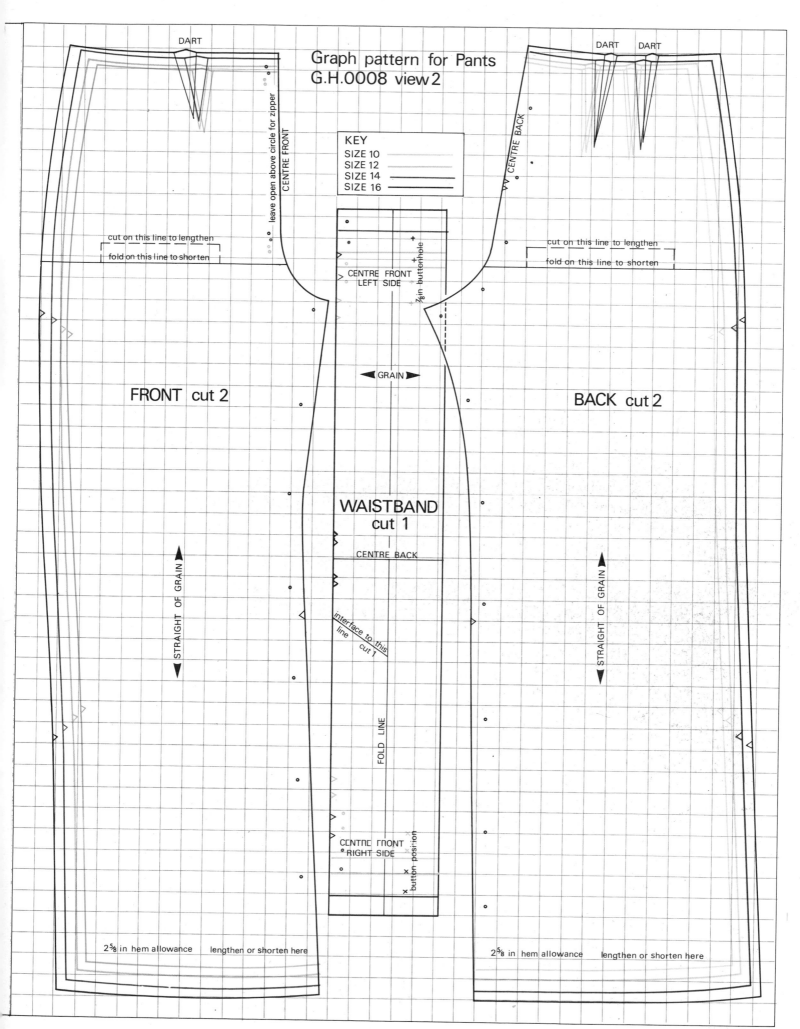

Graph pattern for Pants
G.H.0008 view 2

DART

KEY
SIZE 10
SIZE 12
SIZE 14
SIZE 16

leave open above circle for zipper

CENTRE FRONT

DART   DART

CENTRE BACK

cut on this line to lengthen
fold on this line to shorten

cut on this line to lengthen
fold on this line to shorten

CENTRE FRONT
LEFT SIDE

⁷⁄₈ in buttonhole

◄ GRAIN ►

FRONT cut 2

BACK cut 2

STRAIGHT OF GRAIN

WAISTBAND
cut 1

STRAIGHT OF GRAIN

CENTRE BACK

interface to this
line
cut 1

FOLD LINE

CENTRE FRONT
RIGHT SIDE

button position

2⁵⁄₈ in hem allowance   lengthen or shorten here

2⁵⁄₈ in hem allowance   lengthen or shorten here

1995

1996

Two for sports

Colorful horizontal stripes for her, patterned vertical stripes for him. Both garments have saddle shoulders and a sporting look.

Women's pullover

Sizes

Directions are for 34in bust. The figures in brackets [ ] refer to the 36 and 38in sizes respectively.
Length to shoulder, 27[27½: 28]in, adjustable.
Sleeve seam, 17[17½:18]in, adjustable.

Gauge

5½ sts and 7 rows to 1in over st st worked on No.5 needles.

Materials

Sports Yarn
2 oz. balls
15 [16:16] balls main color, A, purple
4 [4:4] balls contrast color, B, red
1 [1:2] balls each of contrast colors, C and D, yellow and gold
One pair No. 3 needles (or Canadian No. 10)
One pair No. 5 needles (or Canadian No. 8)
Set of 4 No. 3 double-pointed needles

Back

Using No.3 needles and A, cast on 99[105:111] sts.
1st row K1, *P1, K1, rep from * to end.
2nd row P1, *K1, P1, rep from * to end.

Rep these 2 rows for 2in, ending with a 2nd row.
Change to No.5 needles.
Continue in K1, P1 rib working the stripes as follows; 4 rows C, 4 rows D, 8 rows B and 6 rows A.
Rep these 22 rows until work measures 20in from beg, or required length to underarm, ending with a WS row.

Shape armholes

Keeping striped patt correct bind off 4 sts at beg of next 2 rows, then 2 sts at beg of next 2 rows.
K2 tog at each end of next and every other row until 79[83:87] sts rem.
Continue without shaping until armholes measure 6[6½:7]in from beg, ending with a WS row.

Shape shoulders

Bind off 7 sts at beg of next 2[4:6] rows and 6 sts at beg of next 6[4:2] rows.
Slip rem 29[31:33] sts on holder for back neck.

Front

Work as given for Back until armholes measure 5[5½:6]in from beg, ending with a WS row.

Shape neck

Next row Rib 34[35:36] sts, turn and slip rem sts on holder.
Complete this side first.
Bind off at beg of next and every other row 3 sts once and 2 sts 3 times, ending with a WS row.

Shape shoulder

At arm edge, bind off 7 sts every other row 1[2:3] times and 6 sts every other row 2[1:0] times.
Work 1 row. Bind off rem 6 sts.
With RS facing, slip first 11[13:15] sts onto holder and leave for center neck, attach yarn to rem sts and rib to end.
Complete to correspond to first side, reversing shaping.

Sleeves

Using No.3 needles and A, cast on 47[49:51] sts.
Work in rib as given for Back for 3in, ending with a WS row.
Change to No.5 needles.
Using A throughout, continue in rib, inc one st at each end of 7th and every following 6th row until there are 75[79:83] sts.
Continue without shaping until sleeve measures 17[17½: 18]in from beg, or desired length to underarm, ending with a WS row.

Shape cap

Bind off 4 sts at beg of next 2 rows.
K2 tog at each end of next and every other row until 35[37:39] sts rem, ending with a WS row.
Bind off 2 sts at beg of next 10 rows. 15[17:19] sts.

Work saddle shoulder

Continue in rib on these sts for length of shoulder, ending with a WS row.
Slip sts on holder.

Neckband

Join saddle caps of Sleeves to back and front shoulders.
Using set of 4 No.3 needles and A, with WS facing, rib across sts of back neck and left sleeve, pick up and K 11 sts down side of front neck, rib across front neck sts, pick up and K 11 sts up other side of neck and rib across sts of right sleeve. 92[100:108] sts.
Continue in rounds of K1, P1 rib for 1½in.
Bind off loosely in rib.

Finishing

Sew in sleeves. Join side and sleeve seams. Fold neckband in half to WS and slip stitch down. Press seams very lightly under a damp cloth with a warm iron, taking care not to flatten the ribbing.

▼ *Close-up showing the color combination used on the woman's pullover*

Man's Sweater

Sizes
Directions are for 38in chest. The figures in brackets[ ] refer to the 40 and 42in sizes respectively.
Length to shoulder, 28½[29: 29½]in, adjustable.
Sleeve seam, 18[18½:19]in, adjustable.

Gauge
5½ sts and 7 rows to 1in over st st worked on No.5 needles.

Materials
Sports Yarn
2 oz. balls
9 [10:10] balls
One pair No. 3 needles (or Canadian No. 10)
One pair No. 5 needles (or Canadian No. 8)
Set of 4 No. 5 double-pointed needles

Back
Using No.3 needles, cast on 115[121:127] sts.
1st row K1, *P1, K1, rep from * to end.
2nd row P1, *K1, P1, rep from * to end.
Rep these 2 rows for 2½in, ending with a 2nd row and inc one st at end of last row. 116[122:128] sts.
Change to No.5 needles. Commence patt.
1st row K3[6:9], *P2, K10, rep from * to last 5[8:11] sts, P2, K3[6:9].
2nd row P3[6:9], *K2, P10,

rep from * to last 5[8:11] sts, K2, P3[6:9].
3rd row K3[6:9], *P2, (insert needle behind first st and K 2nd st, then K first st and sl both sts off needle tog—called TW2L) 5 times, P2, K10, rep from * to last 17[20:23] sts, P2, (TW2L) 5 times, P2, K3[6:9].
4th row As 2nd.
5th row K3[6:9], *P2, (K 2nd st in usual way then K first st and sl both sts off needle tog—called TW2R) 5 times, P2, K10, rep from * to last 17[20:23] sts, P2, (TW2L) 5 times, P2, K3[6:9].
Rep 2nd to 5th rows until work measures 19in from beg, or desired length to underarm, ending with a WS row.

Shape armholes
Keeping patt correct, bind off 5 sts at beg of next 2 rows, 3 sts at beg of next 2 rows and 2 sts at beg of next 2 rows.
K2 tog at each end of next and every other row until 92[96:100] sts rem.
Continue without shaping until armholes measure 8[8½:9]in from beg, ending with a WS row.

Shape shoulders
Bind off 7[8:8] sts at beg of next 6 rows and 8[6:7] sts at beg of next 2 rows.
Slip rem 34[36:38] sts on holder for back neck.

Front
Work as given for Back until armholes measure 6[6½:7]in from beg, ending with a WS row.

Shape neck
Next row Patt 39[40:41], turn and slip rem sts on holder.
Complete this side first.
At neck edge, bind off 2 sts every other row 3 times, then K2 tog at neck edge every other row 4 times, ending with a WS row.

Shape shoulder
At neck edge, bind off every other row 7[8:8] sts 3 times and 8[6:7] sts once.
With RS facing, sl first 14[16:18] sts on holder and leave for center neck, attach yarn to rem sts and patt to end.
Complete to correspond to first side, reversing shaping.

Sleeves
Using No.3 needles, cast on 49[51:53] sts.
Work in rib as given for Back for 2½in, ending with a 2nd row.
Change to No.5 needles.
Beg with a K row, continue in st st, inc one st at each end of 7th and every following 8th row until there are 77[81:85] sts.
Continue without shaping until sleeve measures 18[18½:19]in from beg, or

desired length to underarm, ending with a P row.

Shape cap
Bind off 5 sts at beg of next 2 rows.
K2 tog at each end of next and every other row until 43 sts rem.
Bind off 2 sts at beg of next 6 rows and 3 sts at beg of next 4 rows. 19 sts.

Work saddle shoulder
Continue in st st on these sts for length of shoulder, ending with a P row.
Slip sts on holder.

Neckband
Join saddle tops of sleeves to shoulders.
Using set of 4 No.3 needles and with RS facing, K across sts of back neck and left sleeve, pick up and K 16 sts down side of front neck, K across front neck sts, pick up and K 16 sts up other side of neck and K across sts of right sleeve. 118[122:126] sts.
Continue in rounds of K1, P1 rib for 3in.
Change to set of 4 No.5 needles and continue in rounds of rib for 3in more.
Bind off loosely in rib.

Finishing
Press each piece under a damp cloth with a warm iron. Sew in sleeves. Join side and sleeve seams. Press seams.

▼*Close-up of the pattern stitch used on the body of the man's sweater*

SEW EASY

Furry batwing jacket

Fur fabric and a leather trim combine to make this cozy jacket top fashion news. Ideal for town or country, the jacket is waist length with batwing sleeves. It can be worn zipped close to the neck or left open if preferred, making it the perfect garment for any winter day.

Measurements

The jacket pattern is cut to fit sizes 10, 12 and 14, and each size is indicated on the pattern by a cutting line of a different color.

You will need:

- ☐ fur fabric 54 inches wide – size 10, $2\frac{1}{4}$ yards; size 12, $2\frac{1}{2}$ yards; size 14, $2\frac{3}{4}$ yards
- ☐ lining 36 inches wide – size 10, $2\frac{1}{4}$ yards; sizes 12 and 14 – $2\frac{1}{2}$ yards
- ☐ interfacing 36 inches wide – $\frac{3}{8}$ yard for all sizes
- ☐ 1 inch wide leather binding – size 10, $6\frac{1}{2}$ yards; size 12, $6\frac{3}{4}$ yards; size 14, 7 yards
- ☐ open ended zipper
- ☐ sewing thread to match fabric and to match leather binding

Pattern graph for Fur Jacket

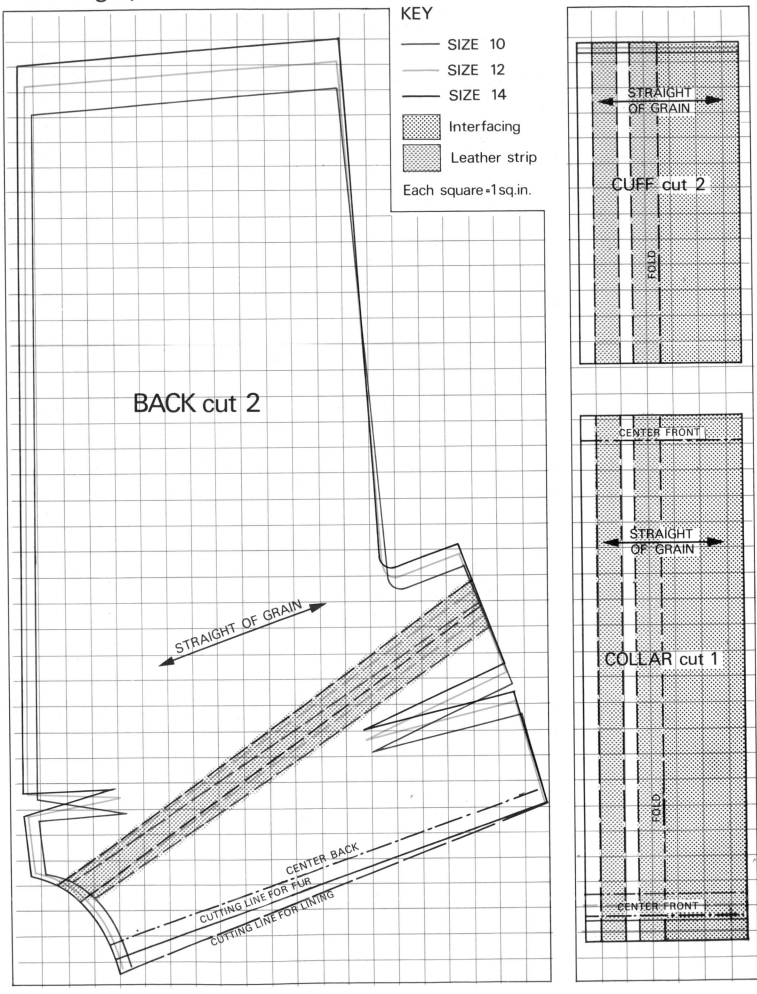

KEY

—— SIZE 10
—— SIZE 12
—— SIZE 14

Interfacing

Leather strip

Each square = 1 sq. in.

BACK cut 2

STRAIGHT OF GRAIN

CENTER BACK

CUTTING LINE FOR FUR

CUTTING LINE FOR LINING

CUFF cut 2

STRAIGHT OF GRAIN

FOLD

CENTER FRONT

STRAIGHT OF GRAIN

COLLAR cut 1

FOLD

CENTER FRONT

2000

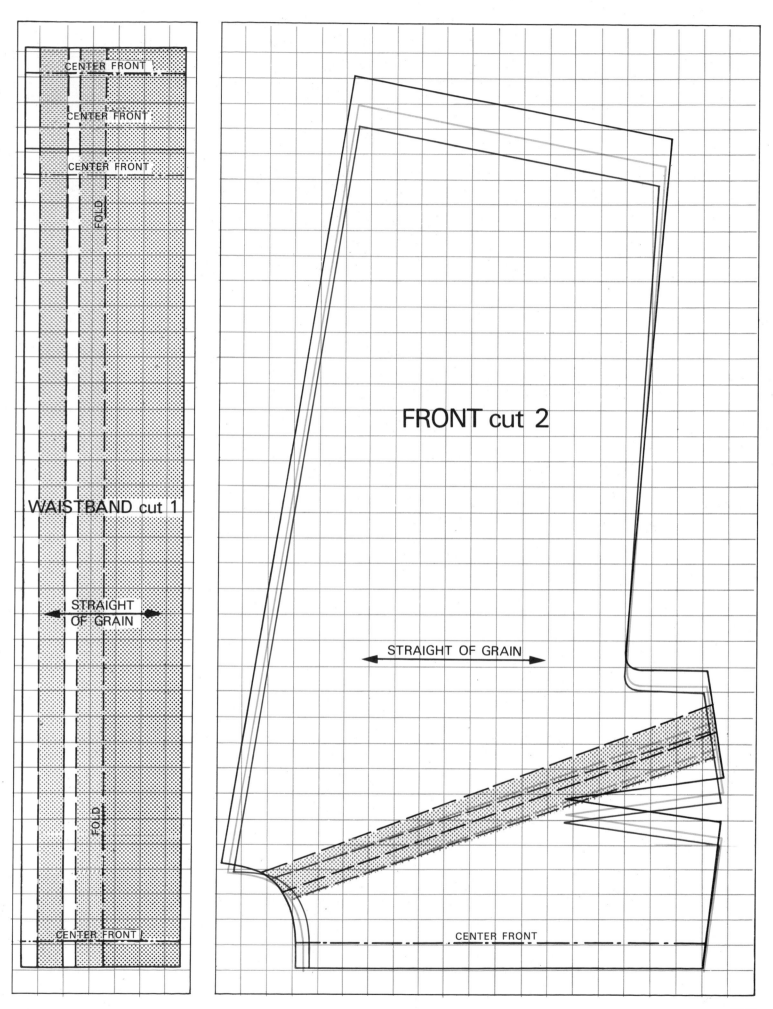

WAISTBAND cut 1

CENTER FRONT

CENTER FRONT

CENTER FRONT

FOLD

FOLD

STRAIGHT
OF GRAIN

CENTER FRONT

FRONT cut 2

STRAIGHT OF GRAIN

CENTER FRONT

2001

Making the pattern

Draw up the pattern to scale from the graph pattern given here. One square represents one square inch.

Follow the black line for size 14, the blue line for size 12 and the red line for size 10. A seam allowance of ⅝ inch is given in the pattern on all edges except on the center front of bodice, collar and waistband where a 1 inch seam allowance is given.

Cutting out

Pin the pattern pieces onto the wrong side of the fabric, following the layout guide and making sure that the pile is running downward from the top to the bottom of each pattern piece.

Mark around the edges of all the pattern pieces with tailor's chalk. Remove the pattern and cut the pieces out with a pair of sharp scissors. Cut the interfacing for the cuffs, collar and waistband to the fold line shown on the pattern pieces. Cut out the lining for the fronts as for the fur fabric, but when cutting out the back piece add the extra ease to the center back as shown on the pattern piece.

Making the jacket

Mark the darts, seam allowances and the positions of the leather strips with tailor's tacks.

Baste the interfacing onto the wrong side of the fabric on the collar, cuffs and waistband.

Pin the leather strips into position as shown on the pattern. Top-stitch down each edge of the leather strips.

With right sides together, baste and stitch the center back seam.

With right sides together, baste and stitch the darts. Cut the darts open and trim away the excess fur so that they lie flat.

With right sides together, baste and stitch the shoulder and underarm seams. On the right side of the jacket, using a pin, tease out any fur caught up in the stitching.

With right sides together, baste and stitch the long edge of the collar to the neck.

With right sides together, baste and stitch the long edge of the waistband to the bodice.

Trim away excess fur on all seam allowances so that they lie flat.

To prevent the fur fabric from catching in the teeth, insert the zipper as follows. Working on the right side of the jacket, mark the center front including collar and waistband with a line of basting stitches. Then trim down the fur on the 1 inch seam allowance.

Lay one half of the zipper on the seam allowance, right sides together so that the teeth protrude over the center front line (Fig. 1). Baste and stitch closely to the teeth; using the zipper foot on the

Luxury-look fur fabric jacket trimmed with bands of leather

machine.

Turn back the seam allowance on center front and herringbone stitch into place (Fig. 2).

Repeat this process on the other half of the zipper. When complete, the teeth of the zipper will be visible down the center front. Turn back and baste the fur for ⅝ inch seam allowance on the sleeve cuff edge and the free edges of the collar and waistband.

Lining

With right sides together baste and stitch down 1 inch at the center back. Press on the wrong side, forming a small pleat. (If there is a center back seam, stitch this before the pleat.)

With right sides together, baste and stitch the darts and press them flat. With right sides together, baste and stitch the shoulder and underarm seams, press open.

Turn center front seam allowance of 1 inch to the wrong side and baste.

With wrong sides together, insert the lining into the jacket.

Baste into position along the neck edge, the top of the waistband and down the

center fronts.

Slip stitch the lining into position down the center fronts.

To secure the lining into the jacket, work a row of stay stitching along the seam lines of the collar and waistband. Now you are ready to fold the collar and waistband in half.

Turn under the seam allowance, baste and then slip stitch to line of machine stitching.

Slip stitch to close the end of the collar and waistband (Fig. 3).

With right sides together, baste and stitch the short edges of the cuff. Trim away the excess fur on the seam allowance.

Run a gathering thread around sleeve edge through both the lining and the fur fabric and draw up evenly to fit cuff. Carefully trim back the fur from the remaining ⅝ inch seam allowances on the cuff.

With right sides together and cuff seam matched to underarm seam, baste and stitch along the leather edge.

Fold the cuff in half and turn in the ⅝ inch seam allowance. Baste, then slip stitch to the line of machine stitching.

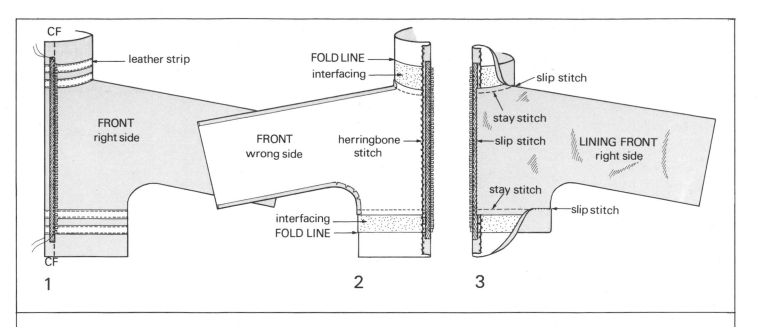

CF
leather strip
FRONT right side
CF

FOLD LINE
interfacing
FRONT wrong side
herringbone stitch
interfacing
FOLD LINE

slip stitch
stay stitch
slip stitch
LINING FRONT right side
stay stitch
slip stitch

1

2

3

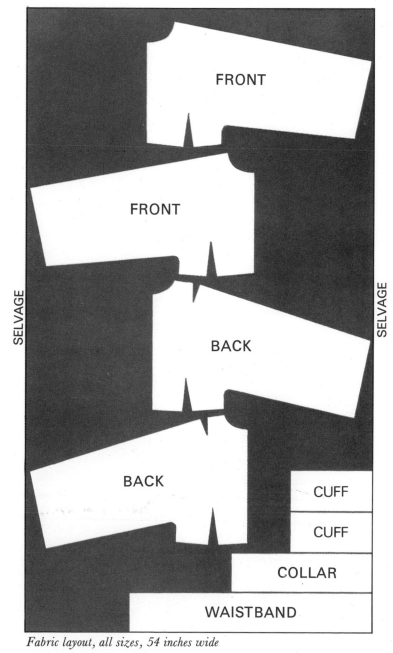

FRONT

FRONT

BACK

BACK

SELVAGE

SELVAGE

CUFF

CUFF

COLLAR

WAISTBAND

Fabric layout, all sizes, 54 inches wide

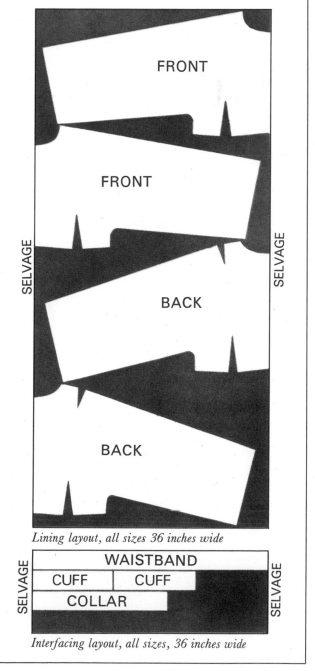

FRONT

FRONT

BACK

BACK

SELVAGE

SELVAGE

Lining layout, all sizes 36 inches wide

WAISTBAND

CUFF

CUFF

COLLAR

SELVAGE

SELVAGE

Interfacing layout, all sizes, 36 inches wide

Shimmering silver

Everyone needs a special dress for special occasions, and what could be more glamorous and feminine than this shimmering, silver evening gown?

The flattering cowl collar is worked as a separate piece

Sizes
Directions are for 34/36in bust.
The figures in brackets [] refer to bust size 36/38in.
Length from shoulder, 64[64]in, adjustable.

Gauge
Each motif measures 12 rows to 3½in and 7 ch5 loops to 4in worked on No.E hook measured after blocking.

Materials
Reynolds Feu d'Artifice 22 [26] 20 grm. balls
One No. D (3.00 mm) crochet hook
One No. E (3.50 mm) crochet hook

Dress

Begin at hem. Using No.E hook, ch217[241].
1st row Into second ch from hook work 1sc, *1sc into next ch, rep from * to end. 216[240]sc. Turn.
2nd row Ch5, skip 2sc, 1sc into next sc, *skip 2sc, ch5, 1sc into next sc, rep from * to end. Turn. 72[80] loops.
Work patt motifs as follows.
1st patt row Ch5, 1sc into first loop, (ch5, 1sc into next loop) twice, *6dc into center ch of next ch5 loop, 1sc into next loop, (ch5, 1sc into next loop) 6 times, rep from * to last 3 loops, (ch5, 1sc into next loop) 3 times. Turn.
2nd patt row Ch5, 1sc into first loop, (ch5, 1sc into next loop) twice, *1dc into each of next 3dc, ch5, 1dc into each of next 3dc, 1sc into next loop, (ch5, 1sc into next loop) 5 times, rep from * to last 2 loops, (ch5, 1sc into next loop) twice. Turn.
3rd patt row Ch5, 1sc into first loop, ch5, 1sc into next loop, *1dc into each of next 3dc, ch5, 1dc into each of next 3dc, 1sc into next loop, (ch5, 1sc into next loop) 4 times, rep from * to last 2 loops, (ch5, 1sc into next loop) twice. Turn.
4th patt row Ch5, 1sc into first loop, ch5, 1sc into next loop, *1dc into each of next 3dc, (ch5, 1sc into next loop) twice, ch5, 1dc into each of next 3dc, 1sc into next loop, (ch5, 1sc into next loop) 3 times, rep from * to last loop, ch5, 1sc into last loop. Turn.
5th patt row Ch5, 1sc into first loop, *1dc into each of next 3dc, (ch5, 1sc into next loop) 3 times, ch5, 1dc into each of next 3dc, 1sc into next loop, (ch5, 1sc into next loop) twice, rep from * to last loop, ch5, 1sc into last loop. Turn.
6th patt row Ch5, 1sc into first loop, *leaving last loop of each st on hook work 1dc into each of next 3dc, yrh and pull through all loops on hook – called 3dc cl -, (ch5, 1sc into next loop) 4 times, ch5, 3dc cl into next 3dc, 1sc into next loop, ch5, 1sc into next loop, rep from * ending with ch5, 3dc cl over next 3dc, 1sc into last loop. Turn.
7th patt row *Ch5, 3dc into top of 3dc cl, 1sc into next loop, (ch5, 1sc into next loop) 4 times, 3dc into top of 3dc cl, ch5, 1sc into next loop, rep from * to last loop ending with 3dc into top of 3dc cl, ch5, 1sc into last loop. Turn.
8th patt row Ch5, 1sc into first loop, *ch5, 1dc into each of next 3dc, 1sc into next loop, (ch5, 1sc into next loop) 3 times, 1dc into each of next 3dc, (ch5, 1sc into next loop) twice, rep from * ending with 1dc into each of next 3dc, ch5, 1sc into last loop. Turn.
9th patt row Ch5, 1sc into first loop, *ch5, 1dc into each of next 3dc, 1sc into next loop, (ch5, 1sc into next loop) twice, 1dc into each of next 3dc, (ch5, 1sc into next loop) 3 times, rep from * to last 2 loops, (ch5, 1sc into next loop) twice. Turn.
10th patt row Ch5, 1sc into first loop, ch5, 1sc into next loop, *ch5, 1dc into each of next 3dc, 1sc into next loop, ch5, 1sc into next loop, 1dc into each of next 3dc, (ch5, 1sc into next loop) 4 times, rep from * to last 2 loops, (ch5, 1sc into next loop) twice. Turn.
11th patt row Ch5, 1sc into first loop, ch5, 1sc into next loop, *ch5, 1dc into each of

next 3dc, 1sc into next loop, 1dc into each of next 3dc (ch5, 1sc into next loop) 5 times, rep from * to last 3 loops, (ch5, 1sc into next loop) 3 times. Turn.

12th patt row Ch5, 1sc into first loop, (ch5, 1sc into next loop) twice, *ch5, leaving last loop of each on hook work 1dc into each of next 6dc, yoh and draw through all loops on hook – called 6dc cl -, (ch5, 1sc into next loop) 6 times, rep from * to last 3 loops, (ch5, 1sc into next loop) 3 times. Turn.

In subsequent repeats, first patt row reads as follows:

1st patt row Ch5, 1sc into first loop, (ch5, 1sc into next loop) twice, *6dc into top of 6dc cl, 1sc into next loop, (ch5, 1sc into next loop) 6 times, rep from * to last 3 loops, (ch5, 1sc into next loop) 3 times. Turn. These 12 rows form patt and are rep throughout.

Continue until 12[13] motifs have been worked. Adjust length here as desired, working more or less motifs.

Change to No.D hook. Continue until 14[15] motifs have been worked from beg.

Left back

1st row Ch5, 1sc into last loop, (ch5, 1sc into next loop) twice, 6dc into top of cl, 1sc into next loop, (ch5, 1sc into next loop) 6 times, 6dc into next cl, 1sc into next loop, (ch5, 1sc into next loop) 3 times. Turn.

Work patt rows 2 to 12 once more, then patt rows 1 to 12 again.

Fasten off.

Armhole and front bodice

Skip 7 ch5 loops and 6sc for underarm.

Attach yarn to 7th sc, ch5, 1sc into next loop, (ch5, 1sc into next loop) twice, *6dc into next cl, 1sc into next loop, (ch5, 1sc into next loop) 6 times, rep from * once [twice], 6dc into next cl, 1sc into next loop, (ch5, 1sc into next loop) 3 times. Turn.

Working on this center set of loops, complete rows 2 to 12, then repeat rows 1 to 5 again.

The collar can also be adjusted to form a softly draping hood

Shape neck

1st row Ch5, 1sc into last loop, *3dc cl into next 3dc, (ch5, 1sc into next loop) 4 times, ch5, 3dc cl into next loop, 1sc into next loop. Turn.

Rep rows 7 to 12.

Fasten off.

Second side of neck

Counting from right to left, skip 1 loop, 3dc, 4 loops, 3dc and 1 loop [twice for second size only], attach yarn to next sc, ch5, 1sc into next loop, 3dc cl into 3dc, (ch5, 1sc into next loop) 4 times, ch5, 3dc cl into 3dc, 1sc into next loop. Turn.

Rep rows 7 to 12.

Fasten off.

Right back

Skip 7 ch5 loops and 6sc, attach yarn to 7th sc. Work as for Left Back.

Hood-collar

Using No.E hook, ch148. Work 1sc into each ch to end. Turn.

1st row As 2nd row on Dress.

2nd row Ch5, 1sc into first loop, *ch5, 1sc into next loop, rep from * to end.

Rep last row 51 times more. Fasten off.

Finishing

Pin out work on large flat surface to shape. Dress measures 38[40] in at hip and 36[38]in at underarm. Length from shoulder to hem 64in.

Press with a warm iron under a damp cloth. Leave until completely dry, then gently unpin.

With a flat seam, sew back and shoulder seams, leaving 8in opening at center back neck.

Using No.D hook, work 2 rows sc all around neck edge and armhole edges. Work 1 row sc on each side of back neck opening, making a small button loop on right back neck. Attach button to correspond. Block out and sew Hood as directions for Dress.

HOME SEWING
Cushion comfort

Giant, squashy cushions make a cheap and attractive alternative to conventional furniture. Make this huge segmented cushion in a riot of contrasting colors for a brilliant effect, or in subtle, toning shades for a restful room. Your children can help you choose the colors they would like for their floor cushion.

You will need:
☐ 1 yard 60 inch wide jersey in navy
☐ 1 yard 60 inch wide jersey in beige
☐ 1 yard 60 inch wide jersey patterned in beige/brown
or
☐ 1¼ yards of the same colors in 36 inch wide fabric
☐ 2 6lb bags bean bag styrofoam pellets

Making the cushion
Draw up a paper pattern from the graph, in which one square equals one inch. Cut one bottom section and one top section from the navy jersey. Cut two navy side segments, two beige side segments and two patterned side segments. With right sides together, pin one long side of a navy segment to one long side of a beige segment. Baste and machine stitch, taking ½ inch seam allowance. Stitch a second seam ⅛ inch in from the first, for strength. Pin the long side of a patterned segment to the beige segment, and stitch in the same way. Continue alternating the segments until a circular shape is formed.

With right sides together, pin and baste the top section in position. Stitch the seam twice, as for the sides. Pin in the bottom section and stitch in the same way around 5 sides. Trim seams and press flat. Turn the cushion through to the right side.

The filling
Styrofoam pellets can be obtained from the following address:
Ain Plastics, Inc.,
65 Fourth Avenue,
New York, N.Y.10003.
As an alternative it is possible to use shredded polyurethane foam. This filling will give you a softer cushion.

Filling the cushion
Use a rubber band to attach one end of a cardboard tube to the bag of pellets. Push the other end of the tube through the unstitched cushion seam and pour in the pellets. Fill the cushion two-thirds full. Pin the final seam and overcast it. It is worth keeping a cardboard tube for removing the pellets when the cover needs to be cleaned, as it will make the whole process much easier.

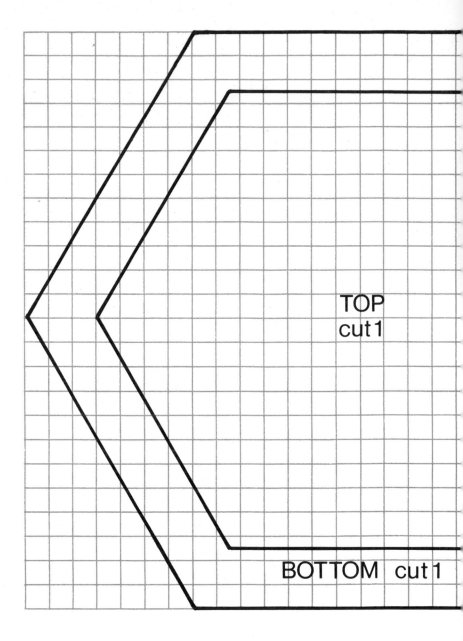

TOP
cut 1

BOTTOM cut 1

graph pattern for floor cush

one square=one inch

seam allowance included

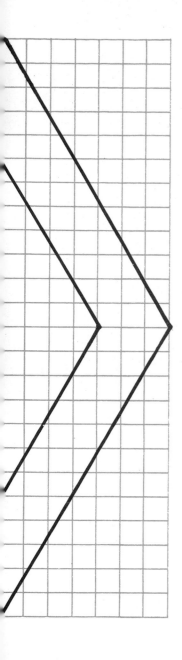

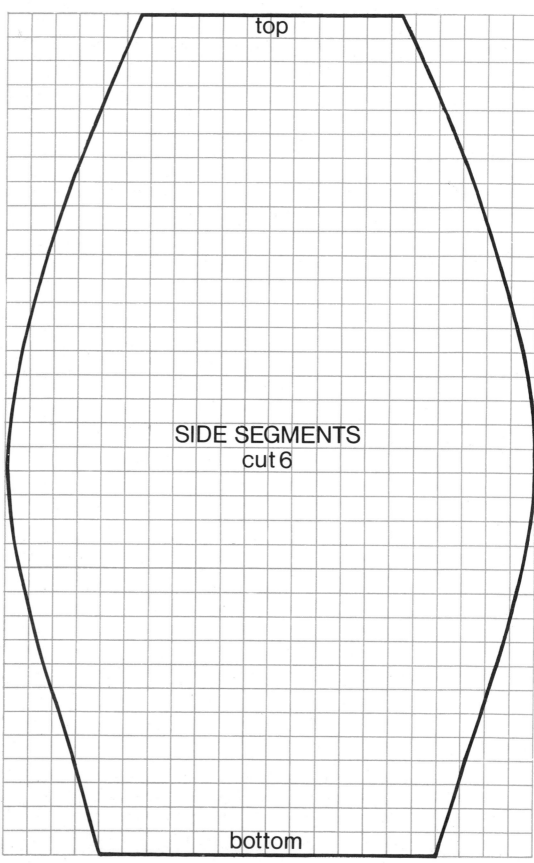

top

SIDE SEGMENTS
cut 6

bottom

2009

Tea cloth with lace insertions

This natural colored linen tea cloth combines angular insertions of machine-made lace with drawn thread work along the hem. Although neither process is a complicated one, great care should be taken with each step to insure neat, accurate results.

To make the tea cloth

Materials required to make the tea cloth measuring 32½ inches square:

- ☐ 1 yard heavy pure linen 36 inches wide in natural color
- ☐ 1 skein D.M.C. 6-Strand Floss in ecru
- ☐ 2½ yards coarse machine-made lace approximately 3 inches wide in natural color
- ☐ 3 yards coarse machine-made lace (same pattern as above) approximately 1¾ inches wide
- ☐ 4 spools sewing thread in natural color (to match above)

To make the tea cloth

Before beginning to work on the tea cloth, try out the stitches required and a sample insertion on a small scrap of the linen. You will find that the warp and weft of the linen, for instance, are

Detail of the lace insert and embroidery

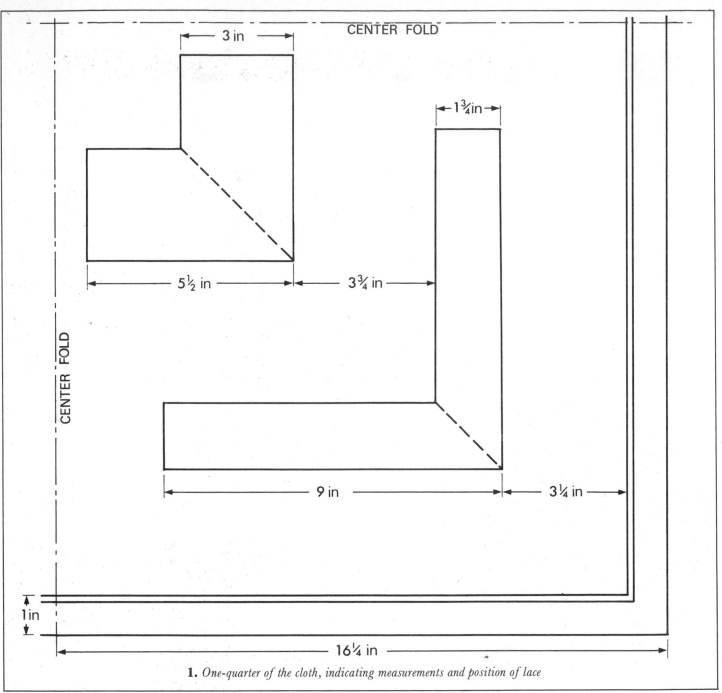

1. *One-quarter of the cloth, indicating measurements and position of lace*

not the same thickness; for the drawn thread work along the hem, more threads will have to be drawn on two sides than on their adjacent sides to make the thread work look even.

Beginning to work
Trim about $\frac{1}{8}$ inch from the selvage edges of the linen and, measuring carefully, trim the fabric to an exact square, cutting along the grain lines. Turn under $\frac{1}{4}$ inch all around the edges, following the grain of the fabric, and baste. Working on a flat surface, find the center of the material by folding it in half horizontally and then basting along the crease, following the grain. Fold the material in half vertically and baste along the crease, following the grain. The material is now divided into four

sections and the center marked. Fold again on the diagonals and baste along these lines. Leave the basting stitches in position until the work is completed as they are essential for positioning the lace accurately.

Making the hem
From the outside folded edge of the fabric, measure inward twice the depth of the $\frac{3}{4}$ inch hem (1$\frac{1}{2}$ inches) on all four sides. With a needle, lift one horizontal thread and snip it carefully with scissors. Still using the needle, carefully unpick this thread working away from the center toward the corners. As mentioned previously, more threads will have to be drawn on two sides than on the other two because of the differing warp and weft. After withdrawing two

threads all around, proceed as necessary to a finished depth of $\frac{1}{4}$ inch. Baste the hem under to within one thread of the exposed threads.

Mitered corners
Before stitching the hem, miter the corners. Working on the wrong side, fold each corner point down so that the point lies where the drawn threads meet. Press each point down, open out and trim the point off diagonally, $\frac{1}{4}$ inch above the crease. Fold the $\frac{1}{4}$ inch turning back on the crease and bring the two newly-made points together (Fig. 2). Slip stitch along the creases.

Drawn thread work
Using three strands of floss in the needle, work on the right side of the fabric from

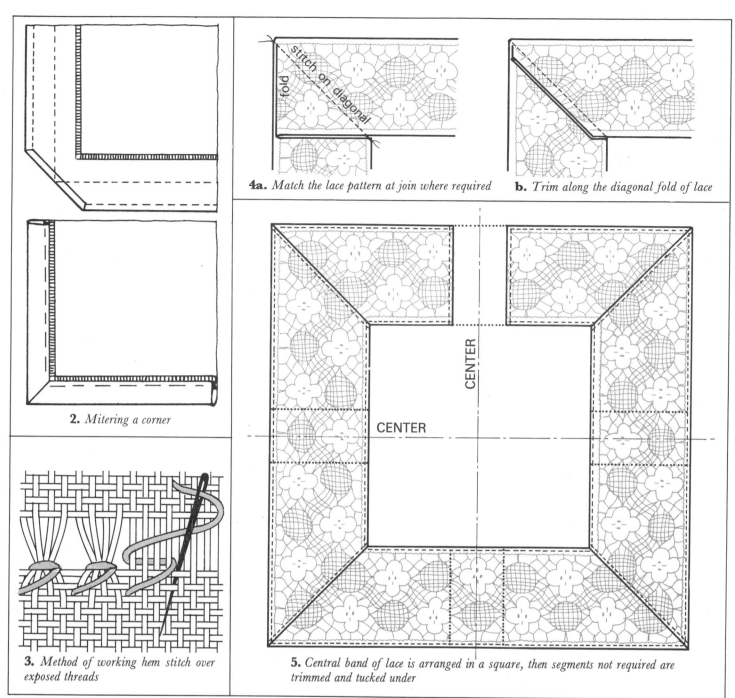

2. *Mitering a corner*

3. *Method of working hem stitch over exposed threads*

4a. *Match the lace pattern at join where required*

b. *Trim along the diagonal fold of lace*

5. *Central band of lace is arranged in a square, then segments not required are trimmed and tucked under*

left to right, with the end of the thread inside the hem. Place the needle in from the right, picking up the appropriate number of exposed threads (approximately 5 threads on two sides and 3–4 on the other two). Pull the needle through and pick up two threads of the turned hem at the back. Make sure that the same two horizontal threads are picked up all along the hem. After working one row of hem stitch along the outer edge of the exposed threads, turn the cloth around and work another row along the inside edge (Fig. 3).

To position the lace

Depending upon the pattern of the lace, it is probably easiest to position the wider lace in a square at the center of the cloth, trimming and folding under those

segments which are not required. Arrange the lace so that the pattern is correctly joined on the diagonal (Fig. 4a). Baste and trim along the diagonal fold before basting the square onto the right side of the cloth (Fig. 4b), taking great care to place the lace onto the exact grain of the linen. Snip each quarter of the lace along the center line, turn under to the required length and baste down (Fig. 5).

Repeat this procedure for the narrower bands of lace, but for these you must first cut the four lengths, making certain that the patterns are evenly matched. Then join the corners on the diagonal. Stitch all the bands of lace to the linen by machine satin stitch, with the stitches just covering the outer edge of the lace. Set the machine at 2·5 for width and 0

for length of stitches. Alternatively, satin stitch may be worked by hand.

Finishing touches

Overcast all the diagonal joins very finely, taking care not to catch up the linen underneath. Then trim away the linen under the lace, close to the satin stitch. Also trim the extra hems of lace and remove all basting stitches. Trim the diagonal joins of lace on the wrong side and make these neat very carefully so that all the threads are caught in and will not fray out, following the design as much as possible.

Dampen the finished cloth and press gently on the wrong side of the work. Spray starch helps to give a fresh look to the finished work.

Patterned evening bag

Old ceramic tiles provide a range of timeless, adaptable designs. The pattern on this evening bag or glasses case is a modification of a traditional Arabian tile, and has been worked in tent stitch.

Materials required

The bag measures approximately $3\frac{3}{4}$ inches by 7 inches when closed.

- ☐ $\frac{1}{2}$ yard 36 inch single thread canvas (14 threads to the inch), or use a remnant measuring 11 inches by 13 inches
- ☐ Pellon measuring 7 inches by 12 inches for stiffening
- ☐ lining fabric measuring 7 inches by 12 inches
- ☐ $1\frac{1}{4}$ yards velvet ribbon $1\frac{1}{2}$ inches wide
- ☐ frog fastening
- ☐ tapestry needle size 19
- ☐ D.M.C. Tapestry yarn in the following colors and approximate quantities: 3 skeins each white, 7139 red, 7317 blue; 1 skein 7746 flesh

Working the canvas

Repeating the design as indicated on the working chart, work in tent stitch (Fig. 1) over one thread of the canvas. Block the completed work and trim the excess canvas $\frac{1}{2}$ inch from the edges of the worked area. Baste the Pellon and the lining fabric to the wrong side of the canvas (Fig. 2).

Binding the edges

Stitch the velvet ribbon neatly along the edge of the worked area (right side), making certain that no unworked canvas is exposed. Join corners as shown (Fig. 3). Fold and baste the outside edge of the ribbon to the wrong side, following the trimmed edge of the canvas. Miter the corners and stitch the ribbon neatly along the edge to the lining fabric.

Finishing the bag

Fold over 3 inches of the bound, lined needlepoint and stitch along the outside edges to close the sides of the bag (Fig. 4). Fold over the top flap to gauge the position of the frog fastening; pin this to the front of the bag and stitch.

▼ *The working chart for the bag shows $\frac{1}{4}$ of the complete design*

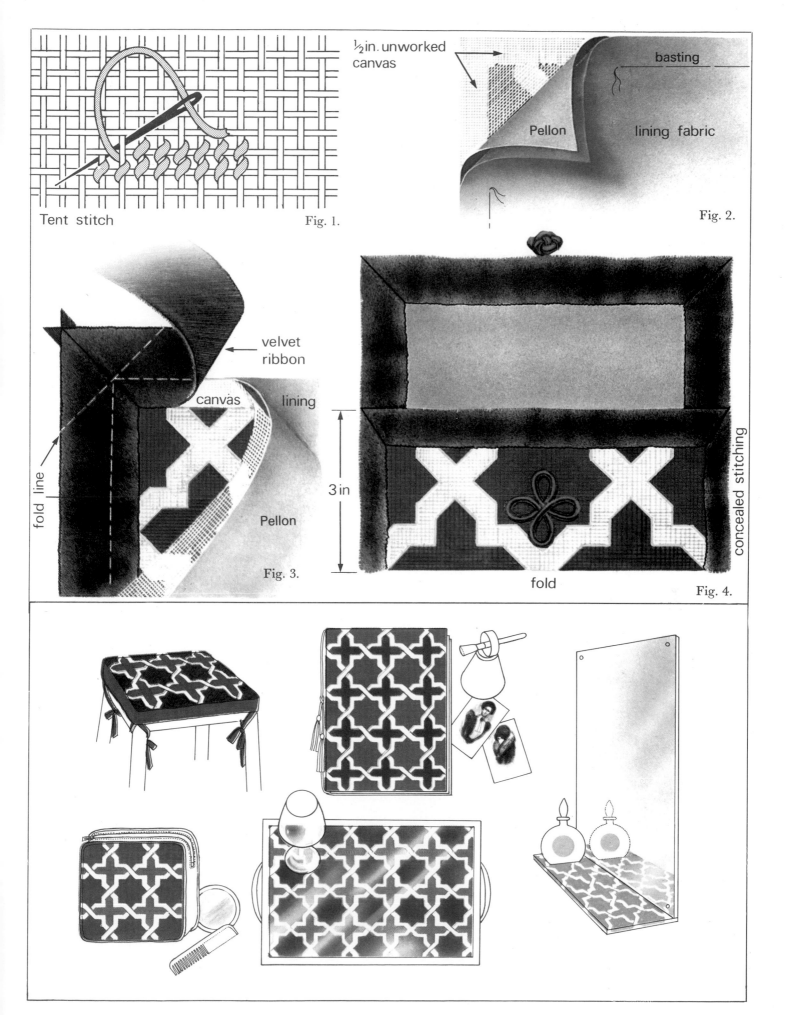

Tent stitch   Fig. 1.

½ in. unworked canvas

basting

Pellon   lining fabric

Fig. 2.

velvet ribbon

fold line   canvas   lining

Pellon

3 in

concealed stitching

fold

Fig. 3.

Fig. 4.

2015

Make a swinging hammock

You will need

1lb No. 15 braided Polythene twine
2 plastic 3in thimbles
1 large netting needle
1½in mesh stick
2 pieces strong wood each 30in by 1½in by ¾in
2 pieces strong rope each about 6ft long

NB The mesh stick determines the size of the mesh and insures that it is all of the same size. It can be improvised from rulers but ideally should be made from plexiglass, 6 to 8 inches long and rectangular in shape.

Thimbles available from:
Atlas Marine Supply Co.,
93 Chambers Street,
New York, N.Y.10007.
Netting needles and mesh sticks are available from:
Fulton Supply Co. Inc.,
23 Fulton Street,
New York, N.Y.10038.

Hammock body

Tie a length of string between two firm points such as the legs of an upturned chair. Load the netting needle by holding it in the left hand with the point upward. Hold the end of the twine anywhere on the body of the needle with the left thumb. Run the twine up the body, around the prong and down the same side of the body to trap the end. Take the twine around the bottom or heel of the needle between the two projections. Turn the needle back to front, still with the point upward, and continue loading by repeating the same process. Load on as much

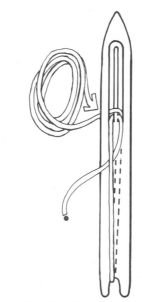

Loading the netting needle

A clove hitch

twine as the needle will comfortably hold and attach the twine to the left end of the string with a clove hitch.

Hold the mesh stick from below with the left hand, thumb at the front. Lay the twine over the front of the mesh stick, taking it around below and up behind the stick to work a clove hitch around the string. This forms the first loop. Cast on 32 loops in all, sliding the mesh stick along as it fills up, but always leaving at least two loops on.

Continued on page 12

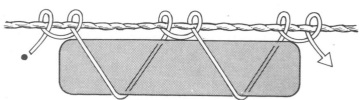

A row of meshes mounted with clove hitches

Continued from page 11
Remove the mesh stick and reverse the work so that the next row will also be worked left to right. Hold the mesh stick immediately below the loops, take the twine over the front of the stick, taking it around below and up behind the stick and out through the foundation loop from the back. Pull the needle downward with your right hand and the mesh stick will be hauled by pulley effect hard up to the

bottom of the foundation loop. With the left thumb at the front and index finger at the back, hold the string and the foundation loop where they cross at the top of the mesh stick.

Throw a loop with the twine across to the left over the foundation loop. Take the twine to the right across the front of the foundation loop, around the back and out to the front through the thrown loop.

Reverse the work at the end of each row and net the required number of rows:

48 rows draw up to 5ft 9in,
50 rows draw up to 6ft,
54 rows draw up to 6ft 6in.

After about six rows, the foundation string can be removed and the clove hitches will fall out, leaving complete meshes.

Slot the first row of meshes onto a loop of string to continue working.

At each end of the work, make one row of 16 extra-large meshes by passing the twine three times around the mesh stick and then taking the needle through two loops before working the knot.

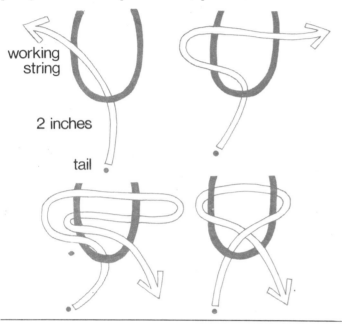

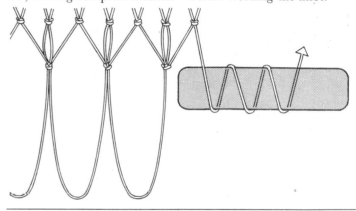

Keeping the left thumb and finger firmly in position until the last moment, pull the knot firm, making sure that it seats correctly around the bottom of the foundation loop and not letting it slip below.

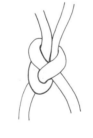

Spreaders

These are the bars of wood positioned at the ends of the hammock. On the broad face of each, mark off 18 holes. Place the outer holes ¾ inch from each end, the next one

in 1 inch along and the next 14 at 1½ inch intervals.

Drill each hole wide enough to take one large end mesh. There will be less wear on the twine if the holes are countersunk at each end.

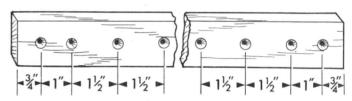

Making the nettles

Leave the hole at each end free and pass the large meshes one through each of the central 16 holes.

Position the thimble with the point toward the spreader at a distance of about 17 inches from the center large mesh.

Using a fully loaded needle, lay the twine around the

thimble and make a netting knot in the end loop. Pass the twine around the thimble before netting into the mesh at the opposite end of the spreader. Pass the twine over the thimble again and net into the next mesh, following the sequence illustrated.

Continue in this manner until all meshes have been knotted.

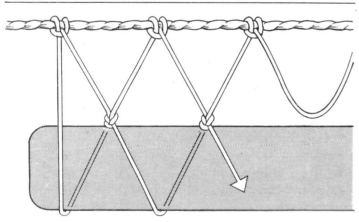

Take care at the beginning of each row not to make the netting knot around the string carried down from the previous

row as well as the first loop. Continue along the row, making a netting knot into each loop.

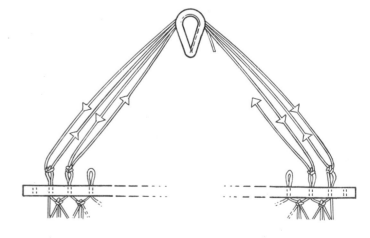

Double a 20 foot length of twine and pass the doubled end through one of the vacant holes in the spreader, pass the double thread around the thimble and through the other vacant hole so that there is a loop of about 6 inches at one side and the remaining length of double twine at the other – this should be at least the length of the hammock.

Work the second spreader in the same way except that the double twine should be arranged so that the loop at one end is at the same side as the double length at the other end.

Continue weaving in this way, but on the next row omit one nettle at each side. Continue to omit the end nettles on each row until only two nettles remain.

Using these as a core, work three flat knots over them with the weaving strands. Fasten off.

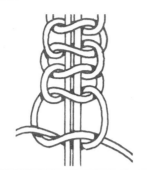
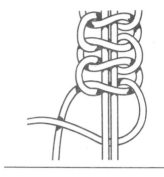

Whipping the thimbles

To insure that all the strands remain in the hollow of the thimble, it is important to cover it with twine.

Use half hitches with the knot positioned over the center of the hollow. Fasten the ends off by weaving into the clew.

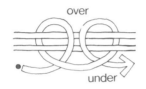

Attaching the ropes

Into the rounded end of the thimble and using the strong rope, work either a netting knot or a round turn and two half hitches.

Bind the end of the rope securely to the main section of the rope by winding very tightly around it with a length of either fine string or thick linen thread.

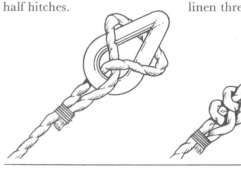

Making the clew

Pass a length of twine around the thimble and position the thimble so that it lies exactly at the center of the length of twine.

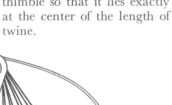

Pass one end over the first double thread (the double thread is called a 'nettle'), under the next and so on across. Weave the other end of the twine from the opposite side over and under the same threads. Pull the ends in opposite directions to draw it tight. Repeat this, weaving over the nettles previously gone under and under the nettles previously worked over. Draw tight. Repeat this process once more, alternating the nettles again in the same way.

Drawing up

Thread the long length of double twine through each mesh along the side of the hammock, then through the looped end of the other doubled thread at the end of the spreader.

Work the second doubled thread in the same way. Draw up the sides to give the required length and dip to the hammock and knot securely in position.

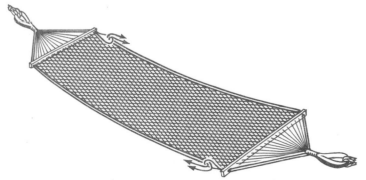

Stripes and dots

Guaranteed to make you feel cheerful, this zingy sweater is striped and dotted for a bright effect.

Sizes

Directions are for 32in bust. The figures in brackets [] refer to the 34 and 36in bust sizes respectively.
Length to shoulder, 22½[23:23½]in.
Sleeve seam, 18in, adjustable.

Gauge

7 sts and 9 rows to 1in over st st worked on No. 4 needles.

Materials

Sports Yarn
2 oz. skeins
4 [4:5] skeins main color, A, white
2 [2:2] skeins each contrast color, B and C, red and navy
One pair No. 2 needles (or Canadian No. 11)
One pair No. 4 needles (or Canadian No. 9)

Back

Using No. 2 needles and A, cast on 122[130:138] sts.
Beg with a K row, work 7 rows st st.
Next row K all sts tbl to form hemline.
Change to No. 4 needles.
Beg with a K row, work 6 rows st st.
Continue in st st and work (4 rows C, 4 rows B, 4 rows A) 3 times then 4 rows C, 4 rows B, *at the same time*, dec one st at each end of next and every following 6th row until 106[114:122] sts rem, ending with a P row.

Commence dot patt

Next row K2 A, *K2 C, K2 A, rep from * to end.
Using A and beg with a P row, work 2 rows st st.
Next row P2 B, *P2 A, P2 B, rep from * to end.
Using A and beg with a K row, work 4 rows st st, dec one st at each end of first of these 4 rows.
Next row K1 A, *K2 C, K2 A, rep from * to last 3 sts, K2 C, K1 A.
Using A and beg with a P row, work 2 rows st st, dec one st at each end of 2nd of these 2 rows. 102[110:118] sts.
Next row P2 A, *P2 B, P2 A, rep from * to end.
Using A and beg with a K row, work 4 rows st st.
Keeping dot patt correct, continue without shaping until work measures 7½in from hemline, ending with a P row.
Continue in dot patt, inc one st at each end of next and every following 8th row until there are 118[126:134] sts.
Continue without shaping until work measures 16in from hemline, ending with a P row.

Shape armholes

Keeping patt correct, bind off 3 sts at beg of next 4 rows and 2 sts at beg of next 4 rows.
Dec one st at each end every other row 6[7:8] times. 86[92:98] sts.
Continue without shaping until armholes measure 6½[7:7½]in from beg, ending with a P row.

Shape neck and shoulders

Next row Patt 28[30:32] sts, turn and slip rem sts on holder.
Next row Bind off 3 sts, patt to end.
Next row Bind off 5[5:6] sts, patt to end.
Rep last 2 rows twice more.
Work one row. Bind off rem 4[6:5] sts.

With RS facing, slip first 30[32:34] sts on holder for center back neck, attach yarn to rem sts and patt to end.
Complete to correspond to first side, reversing shaping.

Front

Work as given for Back until front measures 13in from hemline, ending with a P row. Mark center of work with colored thread.

Divide for neck

Next row Patt to center of work, turn and slip rem sts on holder.
Complete this side first.
Continue in patt still inc at side edge on every 8th row until 8 inc in all have been worked, *at the same time*, dec one st at neck edge on every other row 5 times, then on every 4th row until work measures same as Back to underarm, ending with a P row.

Shape armhole

Still dec at front edge on every 4th row, bind off at armhole edge on next and every other row 3 sts twice, 2 sts twice and one st 6[7:8] times.
Continue to dec at neck edge only on every 4th row until 19[21:23] sts rem.
Continue without shaping until armhole measures same as Back to shoulder, ending with a P row.

Shape shoulder

At arm edge, bind off every other row 5[5:6] sts 3 times and 4[6:5] sts once.
With RS facing, attach yarn to rem sts and patt to end.
Complete to correspond to first side, reversing shaping.

Sleeves

Using No. 2 needles and A, cast on 53[56:59] sts.
Beg with a K row, work 7 rows st st.
Next row K all sts tbl to form hemline.
Change to No. 4 needles.
Beg with a K row, continue in st st, working (4 rows A, 4 rows C, 4 rows B)

throughout, *at the same time*, inc one st at each end of every 10th row until there are 79[83:87] sts.
Continue without shaping until sleeve measures 18in from hemline, or desired length to underarm, ending with a P row.

Shape cap

Bind off 3 sts at beg of next 4 rows.
Dec one st at each end of next and every other row until 29 sts rem, ending with a P row.
Bind off 2 sts at beg of next 4 rows; 3 sts at beg of next 4 rows and 9 sts once.

Neckband

Join right shoulder seam.
Using No. 2 needles, A and with RS facing, pick up and K 70[73:76] sts down left front neck, K up loop between sts at center front and K tbl, pick up and K 70[73:76] sts up right front neck and 12 sts down right back neck, K across sts on holder for center back neck then pick up and K 12 sts up left back neck. 195[203:211] sts.
Next row P.
Next row K to 2 sts before center front, K2 tog, K1, sl 1, K1, psso, K to end.
Rep last 2 rows once more, then still dec in this way on every other row work 4 rows B, 4 rows C.
Continue using A only.
Next row P.
Next row K to center front st, K up 1, K1, K up 1, K to end.
Rep last 2 rows 5 times more. Bind off loosely.

Finishing

Press each piece under a damp cloth with a warm iron.
Join left shoulder and neckband seam. Fold neckband in half to wrong side and slip stitch in place.
Sew in sleeves.
Join side and sleeve seams.
Turn up hem at lower edge and sleeves and slip stitch in place.
Press seams.

2021

Rows
and rows
of rosebuds

The repetition of a simple floral pattern on the shoulders and sleeves of this sheer blouse creates an especially appealing effect. The adaptability of this very feminine motif makes it equally suitable for a border and for larger areas.

The arrangement of the rosebud chains can be varied according to the style of the garment or shape of the article on which it is worked. For instance, several rows of embroidery might be worked at the edge of the sleeves and the work at the shoulders omitted altogether. Or the rosebuds could be positioned either horizontally or vertically along the yoke of a nightgown.

Silk or grosgrain pillows with a floral border might be attractively piled on a bed or chaise. Or for a charming and imaginative gift, make a small sachet of silk. Work the rosebud chains across one side, fill with lavender and trim the sachet with cord or braid. Another idea is to trim the patch pockets on a long wool skirt with several rosebud chains.

To work the embroidery

Green and orange 6-strand floss are required for the blouse shown. Extend the tracing pattern given for the embroidery to include nine flowers in a row. Trace the flowers onto the sleeves in consecutive rows, making certain to align them carefully. Ideally, the embroidery should be worked before the garment is made up, but this is not essential.

Using four strands of floss in the needle, work the stem, sprigs and leaves in green and the rosebuds in orange. The stem is worked in stem stitch and the sprigs are in large chain stitch held with a cross-stitch. The calyx of each flower, its leaves and the rosebud itself are all worked in satin stitch in the appropriate colors.

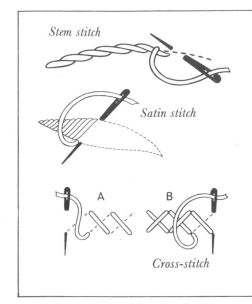

Stem stitch

Satin stitch

A   B

Cross-stitch

Tracing pattern for the rosebuds ▶

2024

New setting for patchwork

Here is a new way with patchwork to make a delightful table setting. The patchwork place mats are sewn onto the tablecloth and are interlined with heat-resistant Milium and bonded fiber fabric to protect a polished table. Matching patchwork-trimmed napkins complete the setting. The materials given here are for making the tablecloth illustrated, but alternative color schemes can be worked out from the quantities given.

To make a tablecloth with a finished diameter of 72 inches and two 12 inch square napkins you will need:

☐ 2 yards 72 inch wide unbleached muslin

☐ 9 yards 1 inch wide bias binding in dark brown

For the patchwork place mats and napkin trims you will need:

☐ $\frac{1}{4}$ yard 36 inch wide plain dark brown fine poplin

☐ $\frac{1}{4}$ yard 36 inch wide plain gold cotton batiste

☐ $\frac{1}{4}$ yard 36 inch wide patterned lawn, predominantly dark brown

☐ $\frac{1}{4}$ yard 36 inch wide patterned lawn, predominantly light brown.

☐ $\frac{1}{2}$ yard 36 inch wide Milium lining

☐ $\frac{1}{2}$ yard 36 inch wide heavy bonded fiber fabric interlining

☐ Tracing paper, stiff cardboard, several sheets of writing paper

☐ Scalpel or craft knife, metal straight edge

☐ Paper glue

Preparing the fabrics

Wash all the fabrics in hot water. Iron while still damp with a medium hot iron. This will prevent any uneven shrinkage after the cloth is made up. Press any creases out of the Milium and bonded fiber fabric interlining and press any creases out of the bias binding. Fold the bias binding in half along its length and press carefully, making a very sharp crease where it is folded. The edges of the bias binding are left folded.

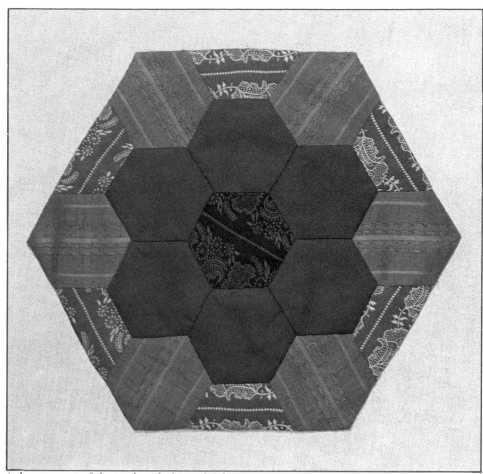

▲ *Arrangement of the patchwork shapes for the place mat*
▼ *The patchwork trim in place on the napkin*

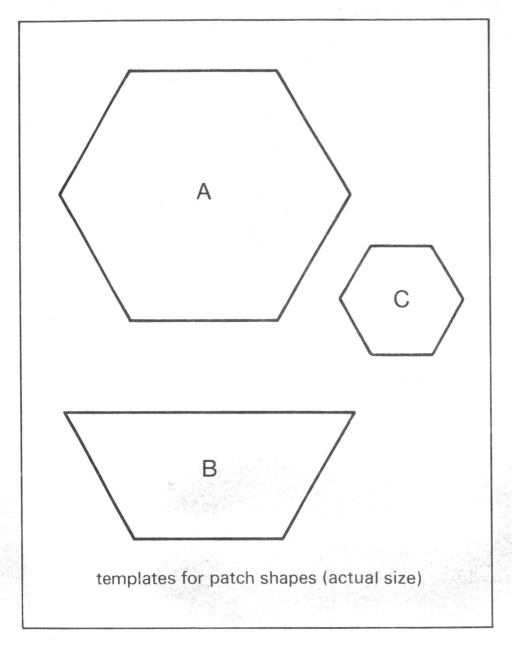

templates for patch shapes (actual size)

1. Cutting out the circular cloth from a folded square of fabric

4a. The patchwork fabric tacked to the paper

Making the tablecloth and napkins

Fold the fabric in half across its width and then in half again to form a square 36 inches by 36 inches.

1. Cut out a circle as shown in the diagram.

2. The napkins are cut from the fabric corners left over. If preferred, the remaining two corners of fabric can be used to make two spare napkins. There will be enough patchwork fabric to trim all four napkins, but an extra 3 yards of bias binding will be required.

Press the squares of muslin carefully, pulling them into shape at the corners if they are at all distorted.

Binding the tablecloth and napkins

3. Baste and machine stitch the folded bias binding over the raw edge of the tablecloth as shown. Press.

The napkins are bound in the same way as the cloth, but the corners are mitered by folding the bias binding. Press the

napkins carefully.

Templates and papers for patchwork

All tracing and cutting for patchwork shapes must be as exact as possible. Trace the templates for patch shapes A, B and C. Glue the tracings to the stiff cardboard and cut along the traced lines with a scalpel or craft knife against a metal straight edge, cutting through both tracing paper and cardboard.

Use the cardboard templates to cut out the papers. Place the templates onto the writing paper and draw around them with a sharp pencil held at a right angle to the paper. Cut out the papers.

Cut 26 papers in shape A, 12 papers in shape B and 14 papers in shape C.

Preparing and making the patchwork

Pin the papers to the fabric with at least $\frac{1}{2}$ inch turning allowance showing around

each patch for shapes A and B and $\frac{1}{4}$ inch turning allowance showing around each patch for shape C.

Cut out around each paper leaving the correct turning allowances.

Tablecloth

Using shape A, cut 12 brown poplin patches, 12 gold batiste patches and 2 dark brown patterned patches.

Using shape B, cut 12 pale brown patterned patches.

Napkins

Using shape C, cut 6 dark brown patterned patches, 6 gold batiste patches and 2 pale brown patterned patches. (If four napkins are being made, double the amounts of both papers and patches.)

4. Pin and baste the turnings on all the patches. Remove the pins.

Join the patches by placing two together, right sides facing, and overcasting one edge with tiny stitches. Join further

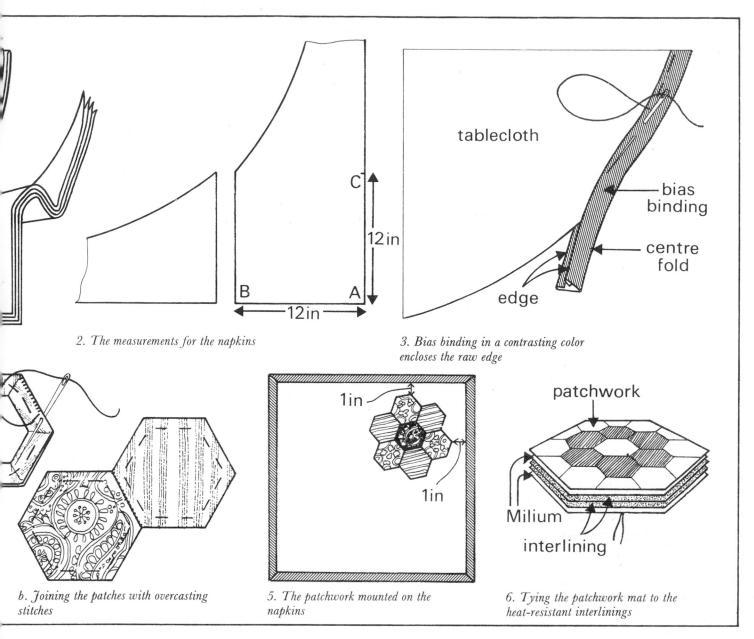

2. The measurements for the napkins

3. Bias binding in a contrasting color encloses the raw edge

b. Joining the patches with overcasting stitches

5. The patchwork mounted on the napkins

6. Tying the patchwork mat to the heat-resistant interlinings

patches in the same way. Follow the detail pictures of the tablecloth and napkin patchwork arrangement.

Press the joined patchwork carefully on both sides.

Remove the basting stitches and pull out the papers. Rebaste the edges, making sure that the turnings are folded under neatly.

Mounting the patchwork

5. The napkins. Place the finished napkin patchwork on one corner of the napkin one inch from each edge, and pin through the central patch. Pin and baste the outer edges of the patchwork, placing the pinheads at the edge and points toward the center to avoid puckering, and keeping the napkin smooth and flat.

Press the patchwork again and slip stitch it to the napkin around the outer edges. Remove the basting stitches.

For each tablecloth place mat, place the finished patchwork face downward on the Milium lining. Draw around the patchwork, remove the patchwork and re-draw the outline $\frac{1}{2}$ inch smaller all around. Cut this shape out.

Using the Milium shape as a pattern, cut two interlining shapes from the heavy bonded fiber fabric.

6. Place the patchwork right side down on a flat surface. Place a Milium shape, silver side down, on top of it. Place two bonded fiber fabric interlining shapes on top and then the other Milium shape, silver side down. Make sure that all the pieces are exactly centered on the patchwork and that there is a $\frac{1}{2}$ inch turning allowance of patchwork showing around the edges.

Baste all the layers together. Turn the layers over so that the patchwork is on top.

Using matching thread, "tie" all the layers together by inserting the needle from the back, through all the layers and out at the top through one of the points of the center patch. Leave at least 4 inches of thread free underneath and return the needle through, close to the first hole, back through all the layers and out again at the back. Tie the loose ends together in a firm knot.

Tie down the corners of all the patches in the same way.

The tablecloth. Place the tablecloth over the table so that the overhang is equal all around. Mark the position of the edge of the table on the tablecloth with basting stitches.

Place two patchwork mats opposite each other, 2 inches from the basted line which marks the edge of the table. Pin the tied patchwork onto the tablecloth, keeping the cloth and patchwork absolutely flat. Baste and then slip stitch the patchwork into place.

Remove all the basting and re-press on the wrong side.

NEEDLEPOINT FOLIO
New chairs from old

An assortment of old chairs found in attics and junk shops has undergone a startling transformation with new seat covers and padded backs in needlepoint. Fresh colors and versatile designs make the chairs decorative enough to hold their own in any company.

To make the chair covers

All the chair seats and backs are worked in satin stitch, using tapestry yarn. A working chart is given for each design and may be repeated as required to fill the area to be worked.

Chair A

The size of the needlepoint panel to be used for covering the seat cushion is 30 inches by 26 inches.

Materials required
- ☐ 1 yard 36 inch single thread canvas (14 threads to the inch)
- ☐ No. 20 tapestry needle
- ☐ D.M.C. Tapestry yarns in the following colors and quantities:
  19 skeins each 7946 orange, 7436 light orange, 7725 yellow; 20 skeins 7139 dark red; 25 skeins 7467 brown

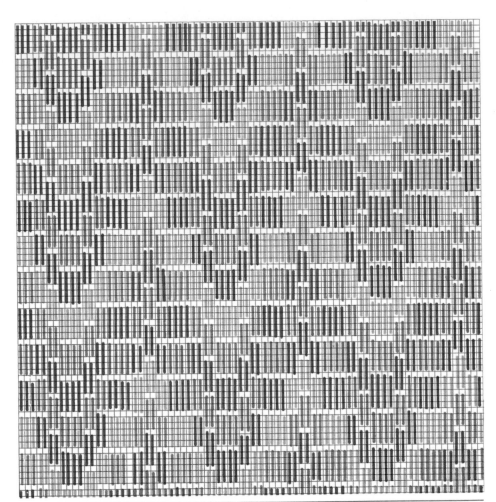

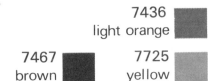

7436 light orange

7467 brown

7725 yellow

7139 dark red

7946 orange

Chair B

The sizes of the needlepoint panels to be used for covering the chair seat and padded back are 18 inches square (seat) and 16 inches square (back).

Materials required
- ☐ ⅔ yard 59 inch single thread canvas (14 threads to the inch)
- ☐ No. 20 tapestry needle
- ☐ D.M.C. Tapestry yarns in the following colors and quantities:
  4 skeins 7467 brown; 7 skeins 7193 pink; 8 skeins 7508 medium brown; 12 skeins 7715 gray

7467 brown

7193 pink

7508 medium brown

7715 gray

Chair C

The size of the needlepoint panel to be used for covering the seat cushion is 20 inches square.

Materials required

- [ ] ¾ yard 26 inch single thread canvas (14 threads to the inch)
- [ ] No. 20 tapestry needle
- [ ] D.M.C. Tapestry yarns in the following colors and quantities:
  7 skeins each 7184 rust, 7725 yellow; 19 skeins 7468 brown

■ 7468 brown

■ 7725 yellow

■ 7184 rust

Chair D

The sizes of the needlepoint panels to be used for covering the chair seat and padded back are 16 inches square (seat) and 10 inches by 14 inches (back).

Materials required

- [ ] ⅔ yard 36 inch single thread canvas (14 threads to the inch)
- [ ] No. 20 tapestry needle
- [ ] D.M.C. Tapestry yarns in the following colors and quantities:
  5 skeins each 7725 yellow, 7168 terra cotta, 7469 brown, 7151 pink; 6 skeins 7606 red

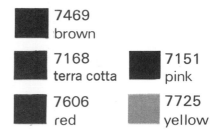

■ 7469 brown

■ 7168 terra cotta

■ 7151 pink

■ 7606 red

■ 7725 yellow

Luxury under foot

This sumptuous rug is specially designed for machine knitters who want to bring a touch of luxury to the living room or bedroom. It is made by a technique which is also useful for making smaller items such as pillows or for trimming garments.

Knitting on a machine is not just a way of meeting the family's needs for classic sweaters, or of making fashionable garments for yourself. There are endless creative possibilities for knitting for the home as well, particularly if your machine can produce weaving techniques. This luxurious rug has a knitted backing, while the dense looped pile is woven in, working with two strands of yarn.

The rug can be worked to any desired width up to the full width of the machine, and it can be made up to any length.

The pillow has been worked with single strand loops. This gives a less dense, more floppy effect, which is also more economical. The rug could also be worked in this way.

Although specific directions are given for the rug illustrated, it can easily be adapted by altering the dimensions, the yarn quality or the length of the loops. It is advisable, however, to use a thicker yarn for the loops than on the backing.

Size

38in by 46in (excluding loops).

Gauge
7 sts and 10 rows to 1 in. measured over plain st st worked in sports yarn. Each loop measures 2 in.

Materials
Backing.
Sports Yarn
6 ounces
Loops.
Knitting Worsted used double 44 ounces
1½ yds. 30 in. wide iron-on backing fabric

Method

Using sports yarn, cast on 200 sts. Knit 4 rows.
Set machine for weaving and put every second needle out of working position.
Make two loops of string, each using a length of about six inches, so that each loop measures exactly two inches. Hook one loop at each end of the needle bed and then hang the cast-on comb onto the loops.
Using 4 strands of knitting worsted throughout, take it over the first needle in the out of work position, down to the comb and hook the yarn under two teeth, up and over the second needle in the out of work position, down to the comb and around two teeth. Continue in this manner along the row. Knit across the row to secure the loops. Knit one row without loops. Put every other second needle (alternate to those in the previous loop row) into the out of work position and hook around the loops as before.
Continue in this manner, alternating a row of loops with a plain row of knitting until the desired length is reached.

Finishing

Run in the ends of the backing yarn and trim the ends of the loop yarn so that they are lost in the pile. Position adhesive backing onto the knitted backing, trimming as required. Press into place with a warm iron. Used in conjunction with a backing of this type, the loops are more secure from catching and ravelling.

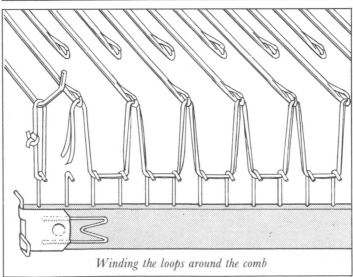

Winding the loops around the comb

Pillow cover-up

This pretty pillow cover would look equally good in a bedroom, lounge or on a patio. Simple to work, it can be lined or just slipped over a ready-made pillow.

Size
15in by 15in, excluding fringe.

Gauge
11 sts and 5 rows to 2in over dc worked on No.D crochet hook.

Materials
Sports Yarn
4 (2 oz.) balls
One No. D (3.00 mm) crochet hook
Pillow form 15 in. by 15 in.
½ yd. 36 in. wide lining fabric
10 in. zipper

Main section

Using No.D hook, ch94.
1st row Skip first 6ch to form edging loop, 1dc into each of next 2ch, skip 2ch, *into next ch work 3dc, ch3, 3dc – called shell –, skip 2ch, 1dc into each of next 24ch, skip 2ch, 1 shell into next ch*, ch16, skip next 20ch, rep from * to * once more, skip 2ch, 1dc into each of last 2ch, turn.
2nd row Ch6 to form edging loop, 1dc into each of next 2dc, * 1 shell into 3ch of shell, ch10, skip 10dc, 1dc into each of next 4dc, ch10, skip 10dc, 1 shell into 3ch of shell*, ch16, rep from * to * once more, 1dc into each of last 2dc, turn.
3rd row Ch6, 1dc into each of next 2dc, *1 shell into 3ch of shell, 10dc into 10ch sp, 1dc into each of next 4dc, 10dc into ch10 sp, 1 shell into 3ch of shell*, ch16, rep from * to * once more, 1dc into each of last 2dc, turn.
4th row Ch6, 1 dc into each of next 2dc, * 1 shell into 3ch of shell, ch10, skip 10dc, 1dc into each of next 4dc, ch10, skip 10dc, 1 shell into 3ch of shell*, ch8, 1sc into all 4 ch loops of previous rows to join them tog, turn, ch2, 8dc into ch8 sp, (turn, ch2, 1dc into each of next 8dc) 3 times, rep from * to * once more, 1dc into each of last 2dc, turn.
5th row As 3rd.
6th row As 2nd.
7th row As 3rd.
8th row As 2nd.
9th row Ch6, 1dc into each of next 2dc, *1 shell into 3ch of shell, 10dc into 10ch sp, 1dc into each of next 4dc, 10dc into ch10 sp, 1 shell into 3ch of shell*, ch8, 1sc into all 4ch loops of previous rows and into corner of previous diamond formed in 4th row to join them tog, turn, ch2, 8dc into ch8 sp, (turn, ch2, 1dc into each of next 8dc) 3 times, rep from * to * once more, 1dc into each of last 2dc, turn.
10th row As 2nd.
11th row As 3rd.
12th row As 2nd.
13th row As 3rd.
Rows 4–13 form patt, noting that corner of diamond is joined tog with 4 loops on every 4th and 9th row.
Rep these rows 5 times more, then 4th–8th rows once.
Last row (joining row) Fold work in half so that RS are tog, ch6, 1dc into last dc just worked, ss into base of corresponding dc on 1st row, 1dc into next dc, ss into corresponding dc of 1st row, *3dc into 3ch of shell just worked, ch1, ss into base of shell on 1st row, ch1, 3dc into same 3ch of shell, 10dc into ch10 sp of row just worked, (1dc into next dc on row just worked, 1dc into base of corresponding dc on 1st row) 4 times, 10dc into ch10 sp of row just worked, 3dc into 3ch of shell on row just worked, ch1, ss into base of shell on 1st row, ch1, 3dc into same 3ch of shell*, ch8, 1sc into corner of diamond and into 4ch loops of previous rows to join them tog, turn, ch2, 8dc into ch8 sp, (turn, ch2, 1dc into each of next 8dc) twice, ch2, ss into base of diamond on 1st row, 1dc into each of next 8dc, rep from * to * once more, work last 2dc as given at beg of row.
Fasten off.

Finishing

Press work on WS under a damp cloth, using a warm iron. Make cover from lining fabric for pillow form allowing ½in seams all around.
With WS of crochet cover facing, join one edge along first dc at side, leaving ch6 loops free for fringing. Insert pillow. Close 2½in at each end of other edge in same way and insert zipper in center.
Fringing. Cut lengths of yarn 9in long. Take 12 strands tog and knot them through double edge loops on seamed edge and through single edge loops along side with zipper closing.
Trim fringe.

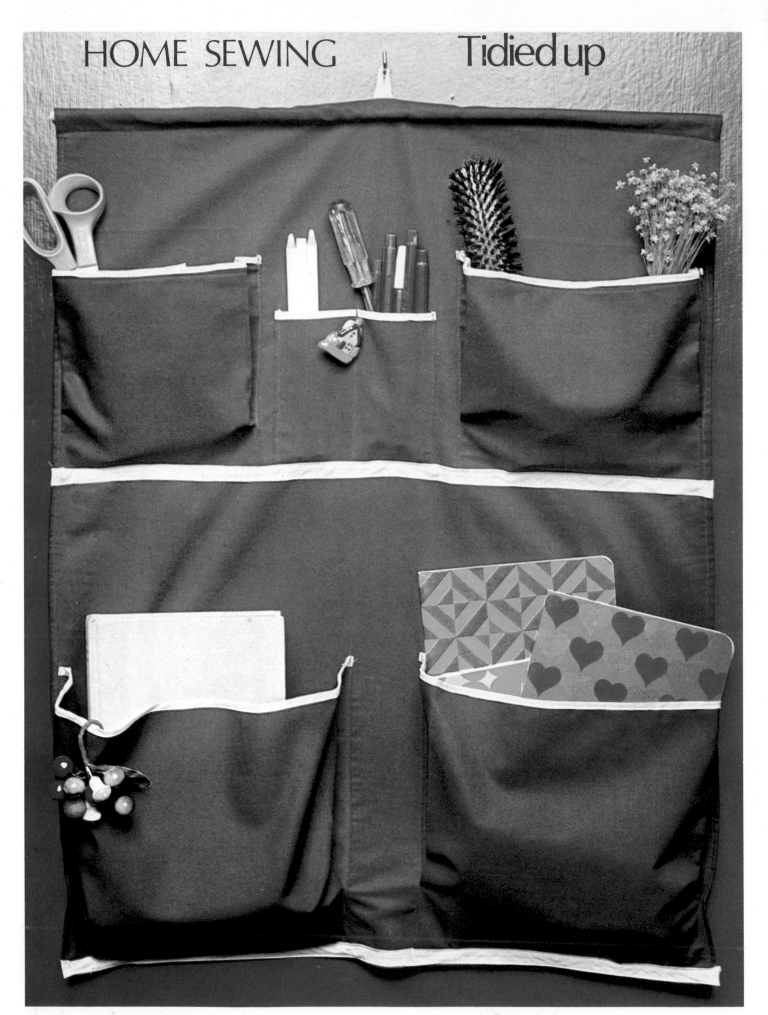

Make this ingenious tidy-all to hang behind a door or on a wall. It is the perfect way to keep safe easily mislaid household items – from brushes to screwdrivers.

You will need:
- ☐ 1¼ yards 36 inch wide navy cotton sailcloth
- ☐ 3 yards white bias binding
- ☐ 1 20 inch length of ¼ inch diameter bamboo or dowel
- ☐ matching thread

Cutting out the pieces

From the navy sailcloth cut one piece 22 inches by 29 inches for the back of the tidy, and for the pockets two pieces each 15 inches by 9 inches, one piece 14 inches by 6½ inches, one piece 11½ inches by 6¼ inches and one piece 6 inches by 4½ inches.

To make the tidy

Turn under and stitch a 1 inch hem on the two long sides of the big piece of sailcloth, then turn under one short side and hem in the same way, using matching thread. Turn under the remaining short side for 1 inch and stitch a ¼ inch hem, leaving a ¾ inch channel to take the bamboo or dowel.

The lower pockets Bind one long side of each of the two 15 inch by 9 inch pieces of sailcloth with bias binding. Turn under and stitch a ½ inch hem on the two short sides of each of these two pieces. With the bound edge uppermost, position the pieces in the lower corners of the backing fabric, so that each piece is ½ inch from the bottom and ½ inch in from the edge.

Stitch the outer side seams, keeping the pockets lined up with the edge and bottom of the main fabric piece. Position and pin the pocket inner edges 2 inches apart. Baste and stitch.

The pocket pleats Make one equal pleat in either side of the two pockets, lining up the top fold with the pocket side seam and keeping the fabric smooth

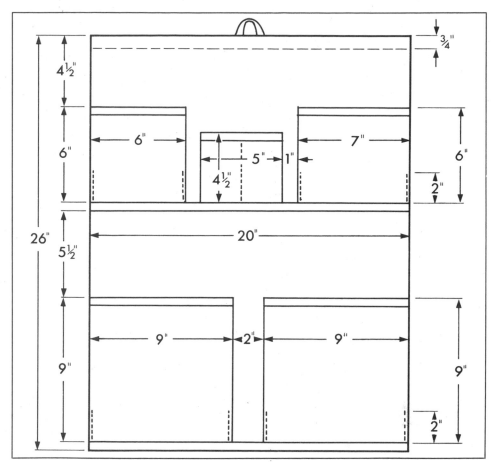
Finished measurements of the tidy, not including side pleats

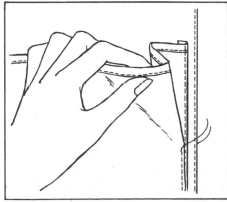
Fig. 1. Making a pleat in the side of a pocket

across the center of the pocket (Fig. 1). The pocket fronts should measure 9 inches across when pleated on either side. Pin, baste and stitch each pleat for 2 inches up the side seam, working from the bottom edge of the pocket.

Place a 21 inch length of bias binding across the bottom of the tidy, to cover the bottom edges of the two pockets. Baste and stitch along the upper and lower edges of the binding, stitching through all thicknesses of fabric. Make neat the ends of the bias binding by turning them to the back of the tidy and stitching securely.

The top pockets Bind one long edge of the 14 inch by 6½ inch piece of fabric with bias binding. Turn under and stitch a ½ inch hem on the short sides. Place this pocket ½ inch from the right hand edge of the backing piece, with the lower, unbound edge 6 inches above the lower right hand pocket. Pin, baste and stitch the outer side seam. Pleat the pocket as described for the bottom pockets, so that it measures 7 inches across when completed. Baste and stitch the inner side seam. Stitch up each pleat for 2 inches, working from the bottom of the pocket. Bind one long edge of the 11½ inch by 6¼ inch piece of fabric with bias binding. Turn under and stitch a ½ inch hem on both short sides. Position this pocket ½ inch from the left hand edge of the

backing piece, with the lower, unbound edge 6 inches above the bottom left hand pocket. Pin, baste and stitch the outer side seam. Pleat the pocket as previously described so that when completed it measures 6 inches across. Baste and stitch the inner side seam. Stitch up each pleat for 2 inches, working from the bottom of the pocket.

Bind one long edge of the 6 inch by 4½ inch piece of fabric with bias binding. Turn under and stitch a ½ inch hem on both short sides. Position this piece centrally between the two top pockets. Stitch the pocket down flat around the three unbound edges. Run another seam vertically up the center of the pocket, to form a subdivision.

Cut another 21 inch length of bias binding and place it across the bottom of the three top pockets. Stitch down as described for the lower strip of binding, turning the ends of the bias binding to the back to make neat.

Finishing off the tidy

Cut a 3 inch length of white bias binding and fold it in half. Place it at the top center back of the tidy and stitch it down very firmly with navy thread, making sure that you do not stitch through the fold. Press the tidy, then slip the bamboo or dowel into the fold at the top.

EMBROIDERY FOLIO

Two more wildflowers

Two more delightful wild-flower panels in cross-stitch from the set shown in an earlier book (page 1932). Work both panels on evenweave linen with 20 threads to the inch. Each panel will measure 25½ inches by 15½ inches when completed and can be mounted or framed.

Materials to make each panel:

- ☐ ⅝ yard evenweave linen (20 threads to the inch, 54 inches wide, ivory)
- ☐ crewel needle, size 8 or 9
- ☐ hardboard or softboard measuring 15½ inches by 25½ inches
- ☐ unbleached muslin or plain cotton for back measuring 15½ inches by 25½ inches

D.M.C. 6-strand Floss

	734	light muscat green
	733	medium muscat green
	732	dark muscat green
	3345	dark almond green
	976	medium chestnut
	975	dark chestnut

Each square represents one cross-stitch worked over two threads.

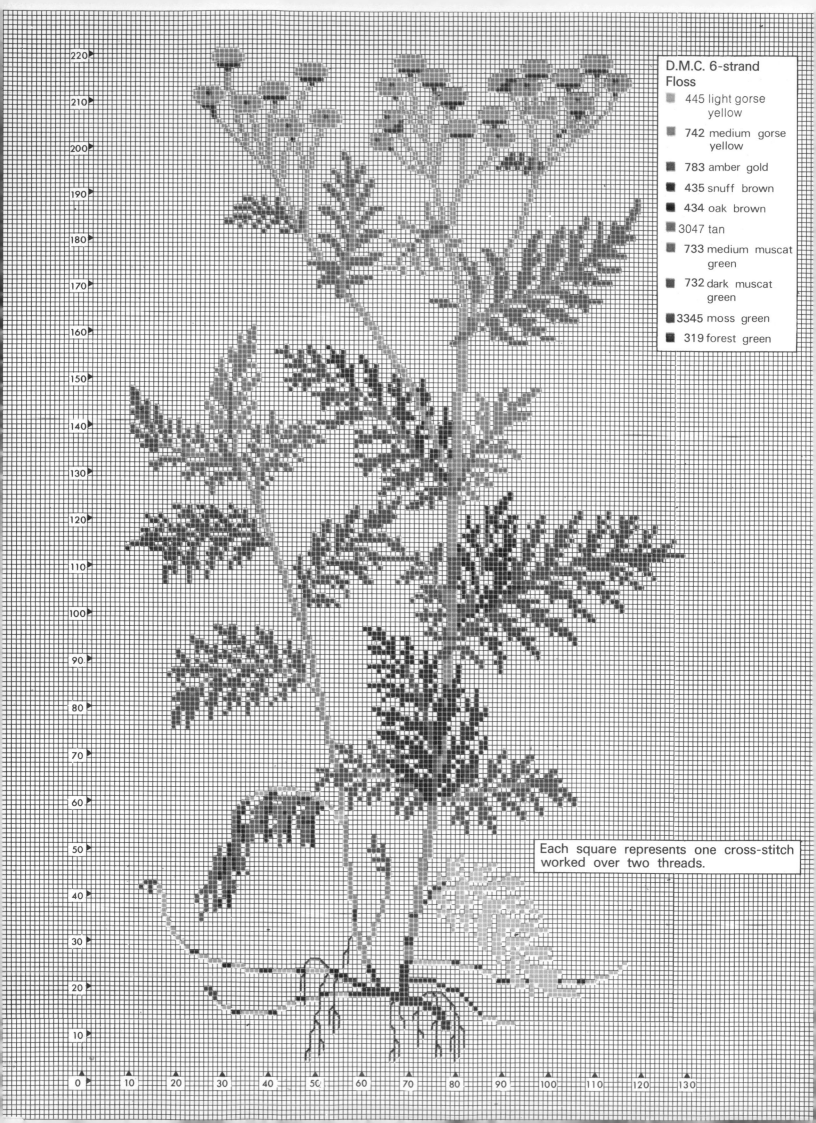

D.M.C. 6-strand
Floss

□ 445 light gorse
   yellow
□ 742 medium gorse
   yellow
■ 783 amber gold
■ 435 snuff brown
■ 434 oak brown
■ 3047 tan
■ 733 medium muscat
   green
■ 732 dark muscat
   green
■ 3345 moss green
■ 319 forest green

Each square represents one cross-stitch
worked over two threads.

For a girl and her doll

Identical outfits for a little girl and her doll. The sleeveless dress has a matching cape – it would be a perfect outfit for a young miss.

Sizes

Child. Directions are for 22in chest.
Length, 16in.
Doll. To fit doll 16in high. The figures in brackets [] refer to the doll's size.

Gauge
6dc and 2 patt rows to 1in worked on No. E hook.

Materials

3-ply fingering yarn
5 [2] ounces
One No. E (3.50 mm) crochet hook
5 [2] tiny buttons
2 [1] yd. velvet ribbon

Dress

Skirt
Using No. E hook,
ch 162[111].
1st row 1dc into 4th ch from hook, *skip 2ch, 3dc into next ch, rep from * to last 2ch, skip 1ch, 1dc into last ch, turn. 53[36]grs.
NB Turning ch and first dc combine with last dc when seam is joined to form one gr.
1st patt row Ch4, *1dc into center dc of gr, ch2, rep from * to last gr, 1dc into last gr, ch2, 1dc into 3rd of ch3, turn.
2nd patt row Ch3, 1dc into first dc, *3dc into next dc, rep from * to end, 1dc into 3rd of 4ch, turn.
Rep these two rows 13[6] times, then 1st patt row once more.
Next row Ch3, *2dc into 2ch sp, 1dc into next dc, rep

from * to end, 1dc into 3rd of 4ch.
Fasten off.
Attach yarn to other end of row.
Next row (picot edge) 1sc into first dc, *ch3, ss into first of 3ch – called 1 picot –, 1sc into each of next 3dc, rep from * to last 2dc, 1sc into each of next 2dc.
Fasten off.

Bodice
Attach yarn to foundation ch and work 1sc into first ch, *1sc into 2ch sp, 1sc into

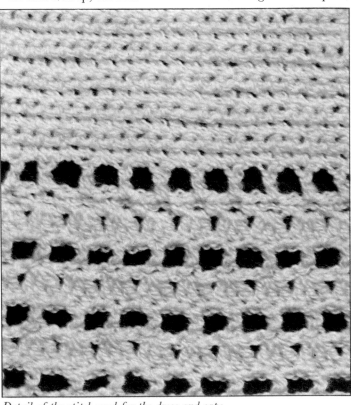

Detail of the stitch used for the dress and cape

base of gr, rep from * to end, 1sc into last ch.
Next row (ribbon eyelets) Ch4, *skip next sc, 1dc into next sc, ch1, rep from * to end, 1dc into last sc, turn.
Next row *1sc into next dc, 1sc into ch1 sp, rep from * to end, 1sc into last sp, 1sc into 3rd of 4ch.
Next row Ch1, *1sc into each sc, rep from * to end, turn.
Rep last row 4[1] times.
Divide for back and armholes
Next row Ch1, 1sc into each of next 22[15]sc, turn.
Complete this side for left back first.
Work 23[12] rows sc.
Fasten off.

Front
With RS facing, return to where work was left, skip 12[6]sc and attach yarn to next st, ch2 to count as first sc, 1sc into each of next 37[29]sc, turn. 38[30] sts.
Work 13[6] rows sc.

Shape neck
Next row Ch1, 1sc into each of next 12[9]sc, turn.
Work 9[5] rows more without shaping.
Fasten off.
Attach yarn to 12th[9th]sc from other edge and complete

to correspond with first side.

Right back
Attach yarn to 22nd[15th]sc from other edge and complete to correspond with left back.

Finishing

Sew shoulder and skirt back seams being careful to match row ends on skirt.
Neck edge. Beg at left back neck edge, work 1sc into each sc along back neck, 1sc into each row end down side of neck, 1sc into each sc along front neck, 1sc into each row end up other side of neck, 1sc into each sc

along right back neck, 2sc into corner and 1sc into each row end of right back opening to waist.
Fasten off.
Work picot edge as given for Dress around neck edge.
Buttonholes. Beg at waist of left back opening, work *1sc into first 4 row ends, ch2, skip 2 row ends, rep from * to neck edge. 5[2] buttonholes.
Fasten off.
Press under a damp cloth, using a warm iron.
Sew on buttons to correspond with buttonholes. Run ribbon through eyelets at waist.

Cape

Using No. E hook,
ch 61[31].
1st row 1sc into second ch from hook, 1sc into each ch to end. 60[30]sc.
2nd row (ribbon eyelets) Ch4, *skip next sc, 1dc into next sc, ch1, rep from * to end, turn.
3rd row 1sc into first dc, *1sc into 1ch sp, 1sc into next dc, rep from * to end, 1sc into 3rd of ch4, turn.
4th row Ch4, *skip 2sc, 1dc into next sc, ch1, 1dc into same sc, ch1, rep from * to last 3 sts, 1dc into last dc.
5th row Ch3, *3dc into next dc, rep from * to last st, 1dc into 3rd of 4ch.
6th row Ch4, *(1dc, ch1, 1dc) into center dc of next gr, rep from * to end, 1dc into 3rd of 3ch, turn.
7th row As 5th.
8th row Ch4, *1dc into centre dc of next gr, ch2, rep from * to end, 1dc into 3rd of 3ch, turn.
Rep 7th and 8th rows 5[2] times more.
Next row As given for last row on Dress before picot edge.
Next row As picot edge given for Dress.

Finishing

Front edges. Work one row sc along each front edge. Press under a damp cloth using a warm iron.
Run ribbon through eyelets at neck edge.

2043

Slimming stripes

This is the pattern that a great many of our readers have been waiting for – a dress in a wide range of sizes up to 44 inch bust. This elegant dress has simple, slimming lines combined with a flattering arrangement of colors.

Sizes

Directions are for 38in bust. The figures in brackets [] refer to the 40, 42 and 44in bust sizes respectively.
Length at center back, 39[39¾:40½:41¼]in.
Sleeve seam, 3¼[3¼:3¼:3¼]in.

Gauge

7 sts and 9 rows to 1in over st st worked on No. 4 needles.

Materials

Reynolds Parfait
6 [7:7:7] (1 oz.) balls main color, A, light brown
6 [7:7:7] balls contrast color, B, dark brown
No. 2 knitting needles (or Canadian No. 11)
No. 3 knitting needles (or Canadian No. 10)
No. 4 knitting needles (or Canadian No. 9)
Stitch holders
6 in. zipper

Back

Using No. 3 needles and B, cast on 177[184:191:198] sts.
Work in st st for 13 rows.
Next row (fold line) K.
Change to No. 4 needles.
Continue in st st, beg with a K row for 12 rows.
Make hem by knitting one st on needle tog with corresponding cast on st all across row.
Make any adjustment in length at this point if required.
Continue in st st beg with a P row. Work 1 row even.
Dec one st at each end of next row and every following 9th row until work measures 4½in from beg, ending with a P row.
Continue dec on every 9th row as before, *at the same time:*
Next row Attach A, K2

A, using B, K to end.
Next row Using B, P to last 3 sts, P3A.
Next row K5A, using B, K to end.
Next row Using B, P to last 6 sts, P6 A.
Continue in this way working 2 sts less B and 2 sts more A on every K row and one st less B and one st more A on every P row until all sts are A, ending with a P row.**
Break off B.
Still dec as before, attach B to beg of next row and rep from ** to **, reading A for B and B for A until 145[152:159:166] sts rem, then dec one st at each end of every following 6th row until 123[130:137:144] sts rem, then inc one st at each end of every following 6th row until there are 135[142:149:156] sts.
When all sts are B, rep from ** to ** once more then continue in A only.
Continue without shaping until work measures 32[32½:33:33½]in, ending· with a P row.

Shape armholes
Bind off 5 sts at beg of next 2 rows.
Dec one st at each end of next and every other row until 107[112:117:122] sts rem, ending with a P row.

Divide for back opening
Next row K53[56:58:61], turn and slip rem sts on holder.
Next row K2, P to end.
Keeping g st edge correct, continue until armhole measures 7[7¼:7½:7¾]in, ending at armhole edge.

Shape shoulders and neck edge
Next row K to last 17[18:19:20] sts, slip rem 17[18:19:20] sts on holder.
Next row S1 1P, P to last 8 sts, turn.
Next row S1 1, K to last 2 sts, turn.
Next row S1 1P, P to last 16[16:17:17] sts, turn.
Next row S1 1, K to last 4 sts, turn.
Next row S1 1P, P to last 24[25:26:27] sts, turn.
Next row S1 1, K to last 4

sts, slip these 4 sts on holder, place rem sts on a spare needle.
Attach yarn to rem sts at center back. Complete as for first side, on 38 and 42in sizes only, K2 tog at beg of first row, and on all sizes reading K for P and P for K.

Front

Work as given for Back to armhole shaping, reversing

Stitch detail showing the interchange of colors

contrast panels, i.e. K to last 2 sts, attach A, K2 A. **Next row** P3 A, using B, P to end.

Shape armholes
Bind off 5 sts at beg of each of next 2 rows.
Dec one st at each end of next and every other row until 107[112:117:122] sts rem.
Continue without shaping until armhole measures 5¾[6:6¼:6½]in, ending with a P row.

Shape neck
Next row K42[44:45:47], turn.
Next row S1 1P, P to end.
Next row K to last 2 sts, turn.
Next row S1 1P, P to end.
Next row K to last 4 sts, turn.
Next row S1 1P, P to end.
Next row K to last 6 sts, turn.
Next row S1 1P, P to end.
Next row K to last 8 sts, turn.
Next row S1 1P, P to end.
Next row K to last 10 sts, turn. Slip these 10 sts on holder and continue in st st on rem 32[34:35:37] sts until work measures same as

Back to shoulder shaping, ending at neck edge.

Shape shoulder
Next row K1, P to last 8 sts, turn.
Next row S1 1, K to end.
Next row K1, P to last 16[16:17:17] sts, turn.
Next row S1 1, K to end.
Next row K1, P to last 24[25:26:27] sts, turn.
Next row S1 1, K to end.
Place these sts on a spare needle.
Return to rem sts at center front and slip first 23[24:27:28] sts on holder.
Attach yarn to rem sts and complete to correspond to first side, reversing shapings.

Neckband

Join shoulders by placing needle holding stitches of right back shoulder with needle holding stitches of right front shoulder. Thread length of yarn into a darning needle and insert K-wise into first st on front needle and slip st off needle. Insert needle P-wise into next st on front needle and draw yarn through, leaving st on needle. Insert needle P-wise into first st on back needle and slip st off needle. Insert needle K-wise into next st on back needle and draw yarn through, leaving st on needle. Continue in this manner until all sts have been worked off. Work second shoulder to correspond.
Press Back and Front lightly under a damp cloth and using a warm iron.
With RS facing, using No. 3 needles and A, K17[18:19:

20] sts from left back holder, K4 sts from holder, pick up and K 12 sts down left front neck, K10 sts from left front holder, K23[24:27:28] sts from center front holder, 10 sts from right front holder, pick up and K 12 sts up right front neck, K4 sts from holder, K17[18:19:20] sts from right back holder. 109[112:117:120] sts.
Work 10 rows st st beg with a P row, working 2 sts g st at each end of every row.
Change to No. 2 needles.
Next row K to make foldline.
Work 11 rows more in st st, keeping g st correct at each end and beg with a K row.
Bind off loosely.

Sleeves

Using No. 3 needles and A, cast on 84[88:92:96] sts.
Work 7 rows st st, beg with a K row.
Next row K to mark foldline.
Change to No. 4 needles.
Work 6 rows more st st, beg with a K row.
Work hem as given for Back.
Continue in st st, beg with a P row and inc one st at each end of second and every following 4th row until there are 92[96:100:104] sts.
Continue without shaping until sleeve seam measures 3¼in, ending with a P row.

Shape cap
Bind off 5 sts at beg of each of next 2 rows.
Dec one st at each end of next and every other row until 50[54:58:62] sts rem.
Dec one st at each end of every row until 20 sts rem. Knitting first and last 2 sts tog to dec as before, bind off rem sts.

Finishing

Press sleeves lightly using a warm iron over a damp cloth. Sew side and sleeve seams. Sew in sleeves.
Fold neckband in half to WS and slip-stitch in place. Sew in zipper.
Press seams.

Suit with a heart of gold

Pants, cardigan and socks in an appealing, bright mix of colors make a warm and practical outfit.

Sizes
Directions are for 20in chest. The figures in brackets [] refer to the 22in chest size.
Cardigan. Length, 11[13]in. Sleeve seam, 7[8]in.
Pants. Inside leg, 11[14]in.

Gauge
5½ sts and 7½ rows to 1in over st st worked on No. 5 needles

Materials
Reynolds Classique, 50 grm. balls
Cardigan. 1 [1] ball main color A, pink
1 [1] ball contrast color B, blue
1 [1] ball contrast color C, yellow
5 buttons
Pants. 2[2] balls C
8 [10] buttons
Waist length elastic
Socks. 1 [1] ball A
Small amounts of B and C
No. 3 knitting needles (or Canadian No. 10)
No. 5 knitting needles (or Canadian No. 8)

Cardigan back
Using No. 3 needles and B, cast on 60[66] sts.
K 6 rows. Break off B.
Change to No. 5 needles and attach A.
Beg with a K row, continue in st st until work measures 6½[8]in from beg, ending with a P row.

Shape armholes
Bind off 4 sts at beg of next 2 rows, then dec one st at each end every other row 4[5] times. 44[48] sts.

Continue without shaping until armholes measure $3\frac{1}{2}$[4]in, ending with a P row.

Shape shoulders
Bind off 5 sts at beg of next 4 rows, then 3[4] sts at beg of next 2 rows. Slip rem 18[20] sts on holder.

Cardigan left front

Using No.3 needles and B, cast on 34[37] sts.
K 6 rows. Break off B.
Change to No. 5 needles and attach A.
Next row K to last 6 sts, turn and slip 6 sts on holder. 28[31] sts.
Continue in st st until work measures same as Back to armholes, ending with a P row.

Shape armhole
At arm edge, bind off 4 sts.
Dec one st at armhole edge every other row 4[5] times. 20[22] sts.
Continue without shaping until armhole measures $3[3\frac{1}{2}]$in, ending with a P row.

Shape neck
Next row K16[17], turn and slip rem 4[5] sts on holder.
Next row P.
Next row K to last 2 sts, K2 tog.
Next row P.
Next row Bind off 5 sts, K to last 2 sts, K2 tog.
Rep last 2 rows once more.
Next row P.
Bind off rem 3[4] sts.

Cardigan right front

Using No. 3 needles and B, cast on 34[37] sts.
K 5 rows.
Next row K to last 6 sts, turn and slip 6 sts on holder. Break off B.
Change to No. 5 needles and attach A.
Next row K.
Complete to match Left Front, reversing shapings.

Sleeves

Using No. 3 needles and B, cast on 36[40] sts.
K 6 rows.

Change to No. 5 needles.
Beg with a K row, continue in st st, inc one st at each end of 7th and every following 8th row until 46[52] sts rem.
Continue without shaping until sleeve seam measures 7[8]in, ending with a P row.

Shape cap
Bind off 4 sts at beg of next 2 rows.
Dec one st at each end of next and every other row until 22[24] sts rem.
Bind off 2 sts at beg of each of next 6 rows. 10[12] sts.
Continue without shaping for length of shoulder shaping on Back and Fronts. Slip sts on holder.
Using C, knit a second sleeve in the same manner.

Left front band

Slip 6 sts from holder onto No.3 needles with RS facing, and attach B.
Inc one st in first st, K to end of row. 7 sts.
Continue in g st until band measures same as left front to neck edge when slightly stretched, ending with a WS row. Slip sts on holder.
Tack band in place and mark position of buttons, the first to come at the first row above lower edging, the second will be on 3rd row above sts on holder, with 3 more spaced evenly between.

Right front band

Slip 6 sts from holder onto No.3 needles with WS facing, and attach B.
Inc one st in first st, K to end of row. 7 sts.
Next row (buttonhole row) K3, bind off 2 sts, K to end.
Next row K2, cast on 2 sts above those bound-off on previous row, K to end.
Continue in g st as for Left Band, working buttonholes to correspond with button positions marked. Do not break off yarn.

Neckband

With RS facing, K first 6 sts of Right Front Band, K next st tog with first st of front

neck, K rem front neck sts, pick up and K 3 sts along side of neck, knitting 2 sts tog at each seam K sts of right Sleeve, Back neck and left Sleeve, pick up and K 3 sts down left front neck, knitting 2 sts tog at join K sts of Front neck and Left Front Band. 62[70] sts.
K 4 rows, working buttonholes as before on 2nd row. Bind off.

Pocket

Using No.3 needles and C, cast on 3 sts.
Continue in g st, inc one st at beg of every row until there are 17[19] sts.
K12[14] rows without shaping.
Next row K8[9], K2 tog, K to end.
Next row K8[9], turn.
Continue on these sts.
Dec one st at beg of every row until 4[5] sts rem. Bind off.
Attach yarn to other 8[9] sts and complete to correspond to first side.

Pants right front

Using No.3 needles and C, cast on 44[49] sts.
K 4 rows.
Change to No.5 needles.
Next row K.
Next row K4, P to end.
Next row (buttonhole row) K to last 3 sts, ytf, K2 tog, K1.
Keeping g st border correct, work 5 rows.
Next row Sl 1, K1, psso, K to last 6 sts, K2 tog, K1, ytf, K2 tog, K1.
Rep last 6 rows 2[3] times more. 38[41] sts.
Work 4 rows more, ending with a RS row.
Next row Bind off 3 sts, P to end. 35[38] sts.
Continue without shaping in st st until work measures $6[8\frac{1}{2}]$in from beg, ending with a P row. Adjust length of pants at this point if required.
Inc one st at beg of next and every following 4th row 4[5] times in all, then at beg of every other row until there

are 49[52] sts, ending with a P row. 11[14]in from beg.**

Shape crotch
Bind off 6 sts at beg of next row.
At inside edge, bind off every other 4 sts, 3 sts, 2 sts and one st respectively.
Continue without shaping until work measures 6[7]in from beg of crotch shaping, ending with a K row.
Change to No.3 needles.
Next row K to mark fold line. Beg with a K row, continue in st st for $\frac{3}{4}$in. Bind off.

Left front leg

Work as for Right Front Leg, reversing all shapings.

Left back leg

Work as for Right Front Leg to **

Shape crotch
Bind off 4 sts at beg of next row, work 1 row even, then bind off 2 sts at beg of next row.
Dec one st at the same edge on every following 3rd row until 33[36] sts rem.
Continue without shaping until work measures one row less than Front to fold line, ending with a P row.

Shape back
Next row K24, turn, P to end.
Next row K18, turn, P to end.
Continue in this manner working 6 sts less on every other row twice more.
Next row K across all sts.
Change to No.3 needles.
Next row K.
Beg with a K row, continue in st st for $\frac{3}{4}$in. Bind off.

Right back leg

Work as for Left Back Leg, reversing all shapings.

Socks

Using No.3 needles and A[C], cast on 25[29] sts.
1st row K1, *P1, K1, rep from * to end.
2nd row P1, *K1, P1, rep from * to end.
Rep the last 2 rows twice more.

Shape toe
Next row Using A, K1, sl 1, K1, psso, K to last 3 sts, K2 tog, K1.
Next row P.
Rep these two rows 2[3] times more. Slip sts on holder to be woven later. Return to where work was left and with RS facing, attach A to the 6[7] sts on second holder, K5[6], K next st tog with first st on first holder, K to end. 12[14] sts. Continue on these sts for 2[2¼]in, ending with a P row.

Turn heel
1st row K6[8], K2 tog, turn.
2nd row P1[3], P2 tog, turn.
3rd row K2[4], K2 tog, turn.
4th row P3[5], P2 tog, turn.
Continue working one more st on every row until all sts are worked off, thus ending with a P row. 6[8] sts.
With RS facing, pick up and K 10[12] sts along side of heel, K6[8] sts on needle, pick up and K 10[12] sts along other side of heel. 26[32] sts.
Next row P.
Next row K1, sl 1, K1, psso, K to last 3 sts, K2 tog, K1. Rep last 2 rows until 14[16] sts rem.
Continue without shaping until work measures same as instep piece to beg of toe shaping, ending with a P row. Shape toe as for other piece.

Finishing

Press work with a warm iron over a damp cloth.
Cardigan. Sew saddle to shoulders. Sew in sleeves. Join side and sleeve seams. Sew on front bands. Press all seams. Sew on buttons. Sew on pocket.
Pants. Join front and back seams. Join side seams, leaving bottom g st borders open. Join inside leg seams. Sew front g st border over back g st border where they were bound-off at top and sew down leg.
Fold over hem at top and thread elastic through. Press all seams. Sew on buttons.
Socks. Sew leg seam. Join seams at sides of foot and weave toe sts. Press seams.

▲ *The sock in pink with boldly contrasting bands of blue and yellow*
▼ *The buttoned opening on the pants leg*

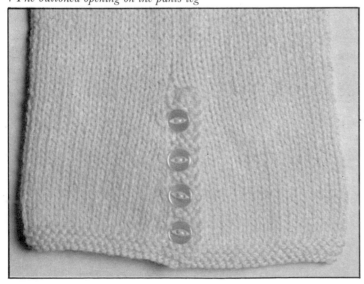

Change to No.5 needles and attach C[B].
Continue in st st, working 6 rows each in C, B, A[B, A, C, B].
Break off yarn.

Divide for heel
Next row (RS) Slip first 7[8] sts on holder, attach C[A], K12[14], turn and slip rem 6[7] sts on another holder.
Next row Inc one st, P to last st, inc in last st. 14[16] sts.
Work 4 rows more without shaping.
Work 6 rows each in B, A, C, B[C, B, A, C, B].

QUICK MAKE
Bias cut skirt

This flared skirt has been cut on the bias of the fabric for a good fit and smooth lines. Here it is made in an even weave plaid, but it would look equally atractive made in a plain fabric without an obvious diagonal weave or nap.

And, as a perfect complement to the skirt, make this delightful, full-sleeved shirt in a toning silk. Turn to page 2053 for complete graph pattern and instructions.

Graph pattern for skirt

notch to side seam

FOLD LINE   C.FRONT   INTERFACING
WAISTBAND cut 1   C.BACK   GRAIN   WRAP

16   14   12   10

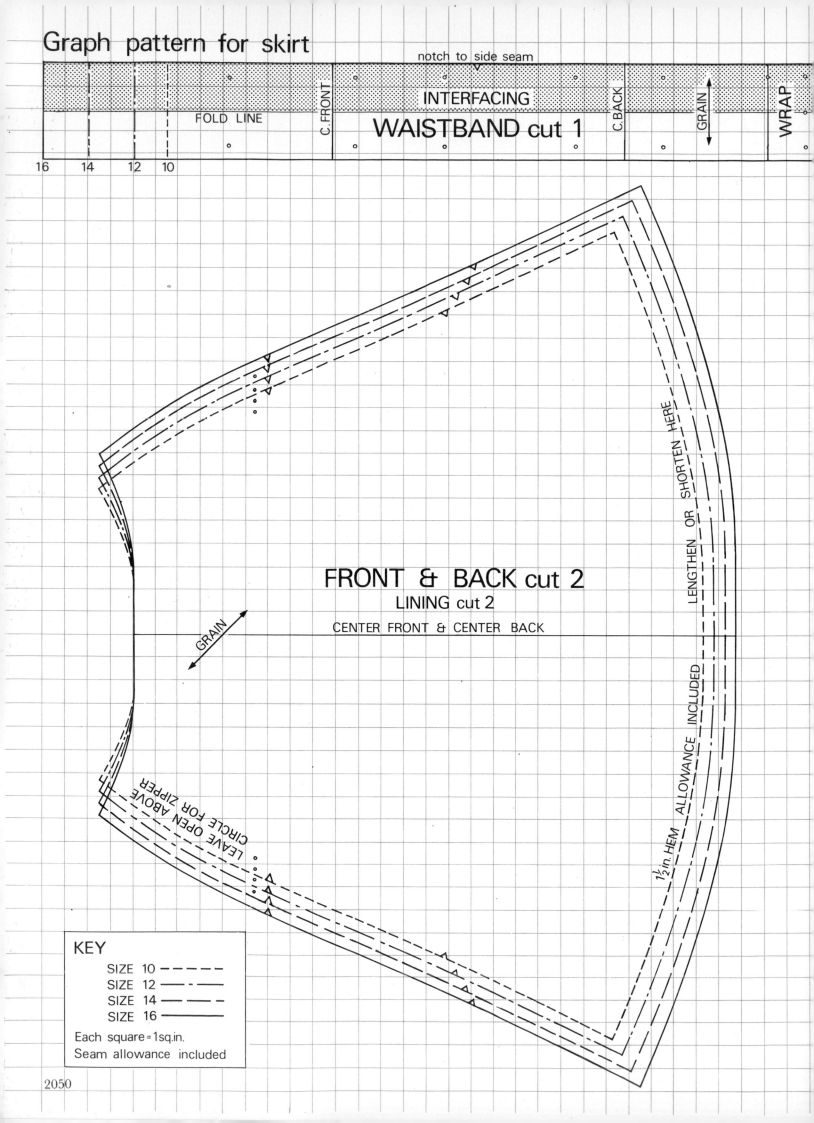

FRONT & BACK cut 2
LINING cut 2
CENTER FRONT & CENTER BACK

GRAIN

LENGTHEN OR SHORTEN HERE

1½ in. HEM ALLOWANCE INCLUDED

LEAVE OPEN ABOVE
CIRCLE FOR ZIPPER

KEY

SIZE 10 – – – –
SIZE 12 –·–·–
SIZE 14 — – —
SIZE 16 ———

Each square = 1 sq. in.
Seam allowance included

2050

Measurements

The instructions given here are for a skirt to fit sizes 10, 12, 14 and 16.

Requirements

- ☐ 2 yards 54 inch wide woven linen, heavy weight cotton, wool or wool mixture fabric without nap for all sizes
- ☐ 54 inch wide lining: sizes 10 and 12, $1\frac{1}{2}$ yards; sizes 14 and 16, $1\frac{5}{8}$ yards
- ☐ $\frac{1}{8}$ yard 36 inch wide woven interfacing for all sizes
- ☐ 7 inch zipper
- ☐ 2 hooks and eyes
- ☐ matching sewing thread

Making the skirt

Side seams and zipper

1. With right sides together, matching notches, baste and stitch the left side seam up to the circle. Press seam open. Insert the zipper in the opening on the left side, following the instructions on the zipper package.

With right sides together, matching notches, baste and stitch the entire right side seam. To make seam edges neat, over-cast by hand or machine. Press seam open.

Lining

2. Make up the lining in the same way as the skirt, omitting the zipper.

With wrong sides together, matching side seams, baste the lining to the skirt at the waist line.

Slip stitch the lining to the zipper tape at zipper opening.

Waistband

3. Baste the interfacing to the wrong side of the waistband along the notched edge. Catch stitch the interfacing along the fold edge. Turn and baste the seam allowance to the inside on the un-notched edge and press flat.

4. With right sides together, matching the notch to the side seam, pin the waistband to the skirt. Stitch through all thicknesses.

Trim the interfacing close to the stitching line. Trim and grade the seam and press it up toward the waistband.

5. With right sides together, stitch the ends of the waistband as shown. Trim the seam and cut across the corners.

6. Turn the waistband to the inside and baste along the folded edge. Slip stitch the waist band to the stitching line. Press.

7. Sew hooks and eyes to the waistband as shown.

Hem

8. Hang up the skirt and leave it over-

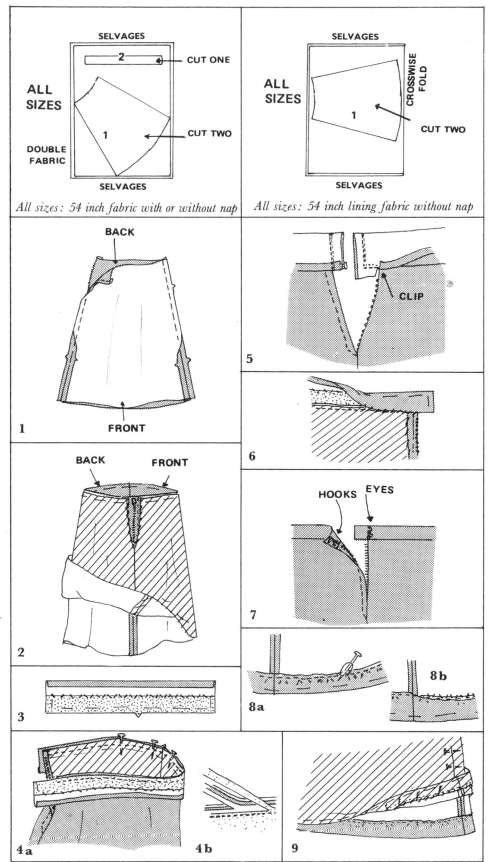

All sizes: 54 inch fabric with or without nap

All sizes: 54 inch lining fabric without nap

night to allow the flare in the skirt to drop. Try on the skirt and mark the hem line. Baste the folded edge. Trim the hem to an even width all around. Finish raw edge with overcasting. Machine gather at the raw edge, pull up the thread to shrink the fullness out. Sew hem with invisible hemming stitch.

Press the folded edge of the hem.

Lining hem

9. Make the lining hem 1 inch shorter than the skirt. Baste the folded edge. Pleat the fullness of the hem. Make the raw edge neat by machine. Slip stitch the hem up.

Classic in silk

This beautifully cut shirt has been specially designed to team up with the bias cut skirt featured on page 2049. However, the design is so versatile that it would look equally attractive worn casually with pants or dressed up for evening wear with a long skirt. The shirt shown here is made in a fine, plain silk, but other soft light fabrics would also be suitable. Printed fabrics which require matching of pattern need extra care in cutting out the material.

Fabrics and notions

- ☐ 36 inch wide fabric, with or without nap: $3\frac{5}{8}$ yards for sizes 10 and 12; $3\frac{3}{4}$ yards for sizes 14 and 16
- ☐ interfacing, $\frac{1}{2}$ yard for all sizes
- ☐ 17 buttons measuring $\frac{3}{8}$ inch across
- ☐ matching sewing thread
- ☐ graph paper for patterns

The pattern

The pattern is for sizes 10, 12, 14 and 16. Draw up the pattern pieces from the graph. The squares on the graph represent 1 square inch. A seam allowance of $\frac{5}{8}$ inch is included on all edges.

Making the shirt

Front

1. Baste the interfacing to the wrong side of the front, having the edge even with the fold line. Catch stitch the interfacing in position along the fold line. Make the raw edge of the facing neat. Fold the facing on the fold line to the inside. Baste and press the folded edge.

Seams

2. With right sides together, matching notches, baste and stitch the side backs to the back and the side fronts to the fronts, easing between the upper notches. Clip the curved edges and press the seams open.
3. With right sides together, matching notches, baste and stitch the shoulder and side seams. Clip the curves and press the seams open.

Collar

4. Baste the interfacing to the wrong side of the collar. With right sides together, matching notches, baste and stitch the upper and under collars together around the unnotched edges. Grade the seam and clip across the corners.

Turn the collar to the right side, baste around all stitched edges. Press flat.
5. With right sides together, matching notches, pin and baste the interfaced edge of the collar to the shirt neck edge, leaving the upper collar free.
Stitch the entire neck seam. Grade the seam and press toward the collar.
Turn the seam allowance on the upper collar to the inside. Hem to stitching line and press. Top-stitch around the collar edge if desired.

Sleeve opening

6. Cut two pieces of fabric measuring 3 inches square. With right sides together, pin and baste the pieces to the sleeves centrally over the slash line. Stitch $\frac{1}{4}$ inch away from the slash line to the circle as shown. Slash to the circle as shown. Turn the piece to the inside. Baste around all edges and press flat.

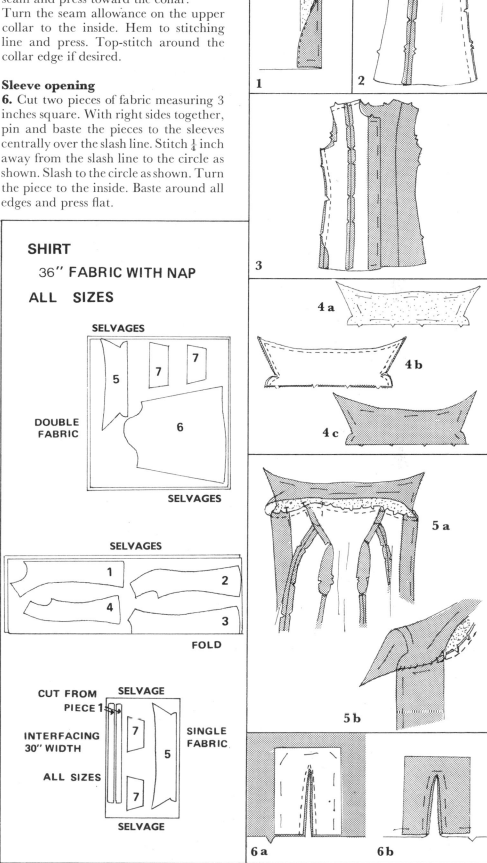

SHIRT

36″ FABRIC WITH NAP

ALL SIZES

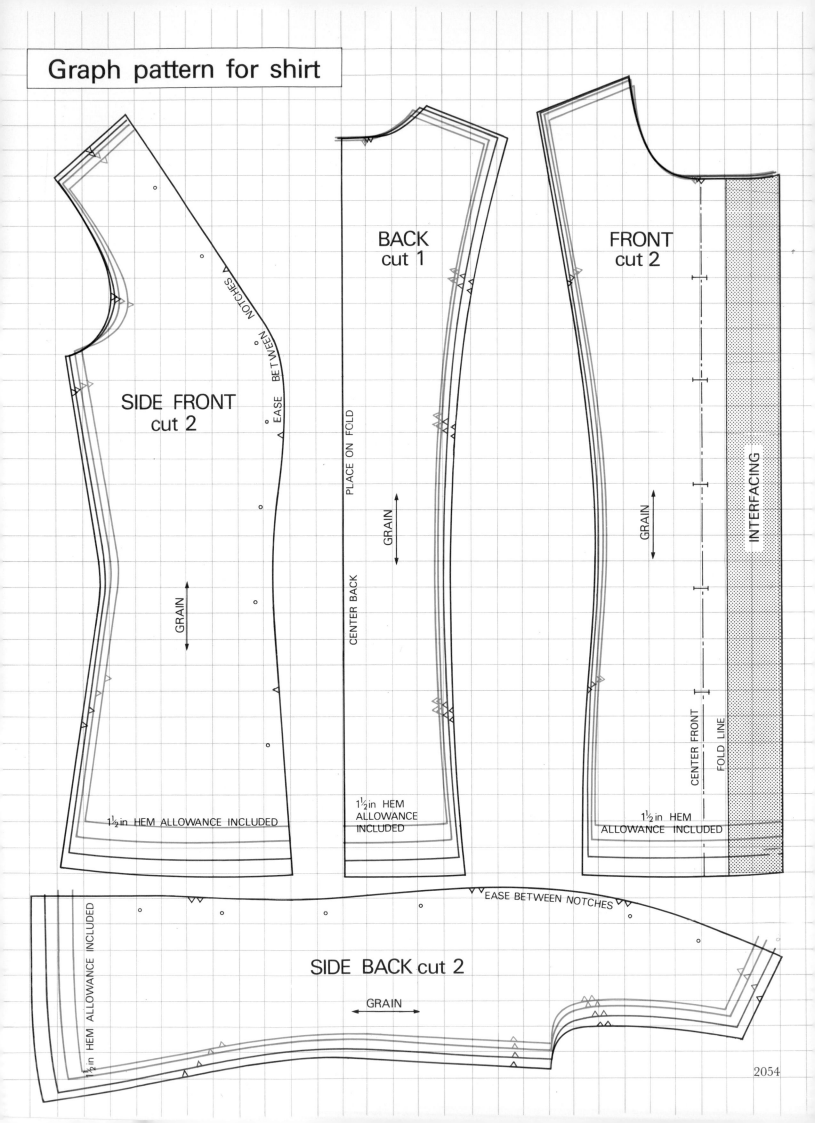

Graph pattern for shirt

SIDE FRONT
cut 2

EASE BETWEEN NOTCHES

GRAIN

1½ in HEM ALLOWANCE INCLUDED

BACK
cut 1

PLACE ON FOLD

CENTER BACK

GRAIN

1½ in HEM
ALLOWANCE
INCLUDED

FRONT
cut 2

GRAIN

INTERFACING

CENTER FRONT

FOLD LINE

1½ in HEM
ALLOWANCE INCLUDED

SIDE BACK cut 2

EASE BETWEEN NOTCHES

1½ in HEM ALLOWANCE INCLUDED

GRAIN

2054

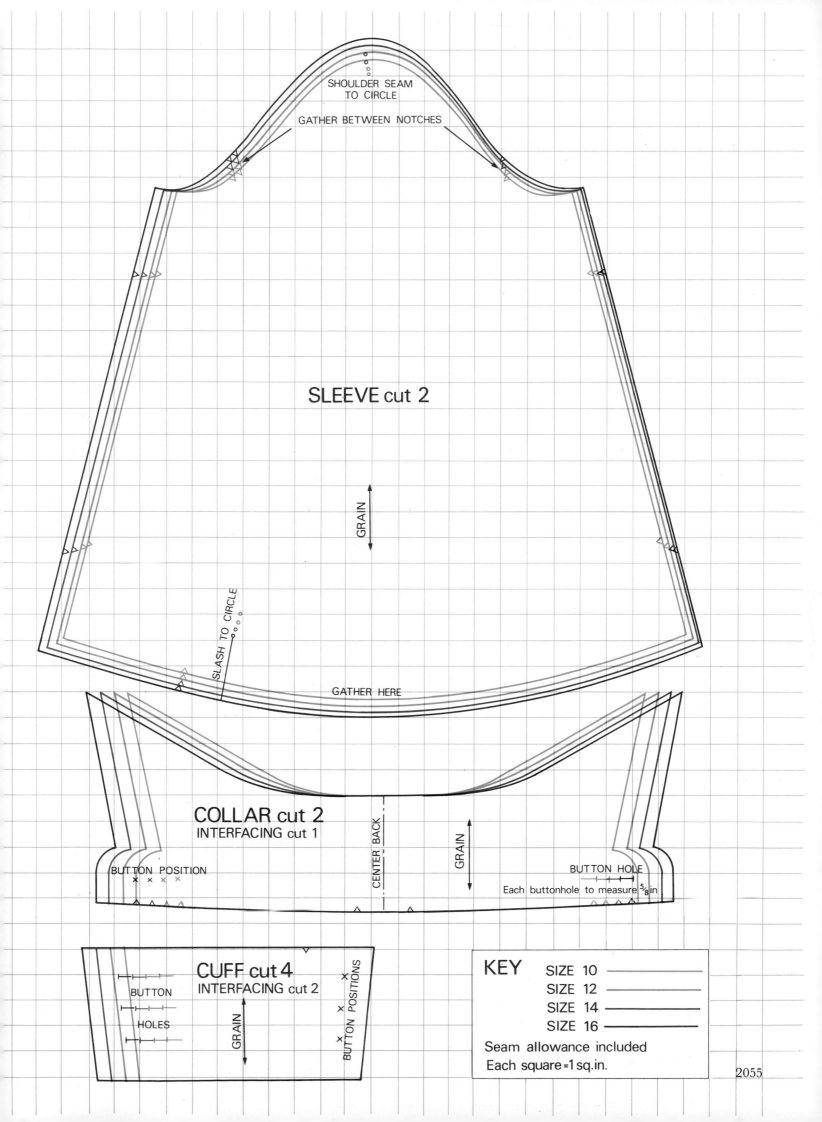

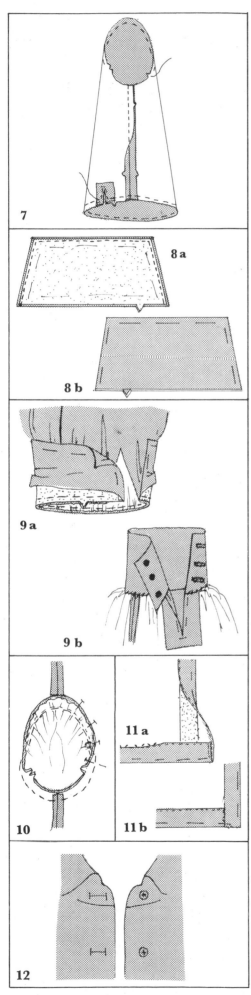

Sleeve

7. With right sides together, matching notches, baste and stitch the underarm seam. Press open. Run a row of gathers between the notches on the sleeve head and around the lower edge of the sleeve as shown.

Cuff

8. Baste the interfacing to the wrong side of the cuff. With right sides together, matching notches, baste and stitch the cuffs together around the unnotched edges. Grade the seam and turn the cuff to the right side. Baste around the stitched edges and press flat.

9. With right sides together, matching notches and the edge of the cuff to the sleeve, draw up the gathers to fit the cuff. Baste and stitch the interfaced side of the cuff to the sleeve, leaving the other side of the cuff free. Grade the seam and press it up toward the cuff. Turn the seam allowance on the unstitched cuff to the inside, and hem to the stitching line. Top-stitch around cuff edges if desired. Mark three or four buttonholes, each ½ inch wide and evenly spaced, on the cuff, working ½ inch in from the lower edge of the cuff.

Work hand or machine stitched buttonholes and sew the buttons into position.

Sewing in the sleeve

10. With right sides together, matching notches and underarm seam, pin the sleeve to the armhole, drawing the gathers up evenly to fit the armhole. Baste and stitch with the sleeve uppermost. Trim the seam and clip the curves. Make the edge neat and press the seam toward the sleeve.

Hem

11. Turn the facing out, turn up the hem and baste along the fold line. Make the raw edge of the hem neat with machine overcasting. Stitch the hem with invisible hemming stitch.

Turn the facing to the inside and slip stitch to the hem. Press flat.

Buttonholes and buttons

12. On the collar, mark a ½ inch buttonhole ¾ inch in from the edge. Mark 8 more buttonholes down the right front, ¾ inch in from the fold line.

Work hand or machine stitched buttonholes. Sew the buttons to the center front on the left side under the buttonholes.

Romantic rose

Appliqué, quilting and areas of stitchery combine to make this wall panel an interesting variation on the floral form as a motif for embroidery. Pastel shades against a white background enhance the romantic quality of this flower, yet there are sufficient elements which provide texture and relief to give the panel impact.

The flower is first worked as a piece of English quilting, and then certain lines are accentuated with chain stitch and couching. The background is fundamentally a free-flowing arrangement of overlapping leaves shadowed with French knots and Cretan stitch.

Materials required:

To make a panel 16½ inches by 23½ inches.

- ☐ ¾ yard white medium weight cotton, 36 inches wide, as backing fabric
- ☐ ¾ yard pale pink nylon chiffon, 36 inches wide (or 1½ yards if two layers of fabric are used)
- ☐ Dacron wadding measuring approximately 8 inches square
- ☐ ¼ yard mauve nylon net
- ☐ ¼ yard pale green chiffon, or a green chiffon headscarf
- ☐ two large sheets of tissue paper, measuring at least 16½ inches by 23½ inches
- ☐ 6-strand floss in mauve and pink shades (choose colors to complement fabrics)
- ☐ pearl cotton in green
- ☐ a small quantity of gold thread, fine enough to fit through a needle
- ☐ small gold and green beads

Method of working

1. Baste a rectangular outline 16½ inches by 23½ inches on the white cotton backing fabric in a color dark enough to show through the chiffon.

2. Within the basted outline, indicate the position of the flower on the backing fabric with four pins.

3. Place the wadding over this area and pin down.

4. Cover the wadding with the pink chiffon and baste through all the layers to hold the wadding in place.

5. Using the tracing pattern of the flower, make a tracing of the main lines on tissue paper. Pin this over the wadding and baste the lines in a pale color thread through all the layers of fabric. Tear the paper away.

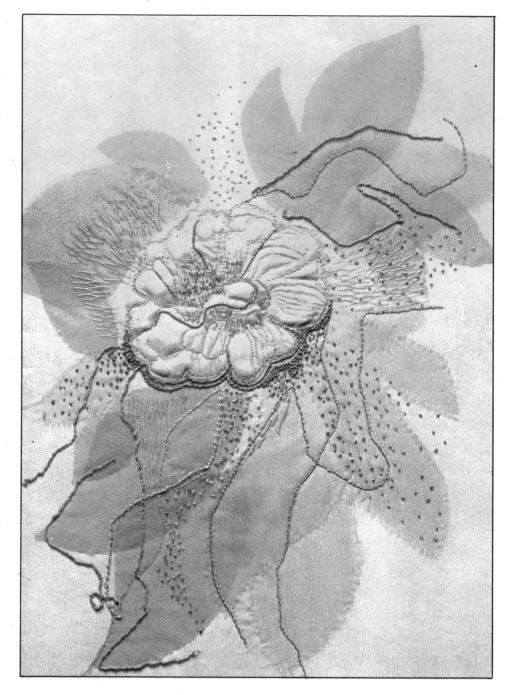

6. Next, quilt the flower, using the main lines for guidance and adding the others freehand. Outline the petals in small couching, using two strands of floss couched down by one strand. The inner lines are worked in broken back stitch, and some of the heavy lines are in twisted chain stitch. All are in self color, using two strands of floss.

7. Carefully lift the chiffon background fabric up and cut away the extra wadding from around the edge of the flower.

8. Add a couched line around the top edge of the petals, using mauve floss. Two lines of twisted chain stitch are worked along the outer edge of the lower two petals, and a little color is added in the thicker lines.

(Note: the flower can be completed at this stage or left until the background

has been completed.)

9. Cut out tissue paper patterns for the leaves, then cut out the shapes in net and chiffon. Position the green chiffon shapes, then place the mauve net over the top. Baste or pin in place. Stitch in position with tiny stab stitches near the edges every half inch or so, using a color to match the background or invisible nylon thread.

10. To make the background, work couching or twisted chain stitches for the heavier lines, using mauve thread at the bottom and pink at the top, as indicated on the graph pattern.

French knots and Cretan stitch add flow and texture to the background. For all the lines radiating from the flower at the right, bottom left and top left, work Cretan stitch in one strand of

tracing pattern
for flower

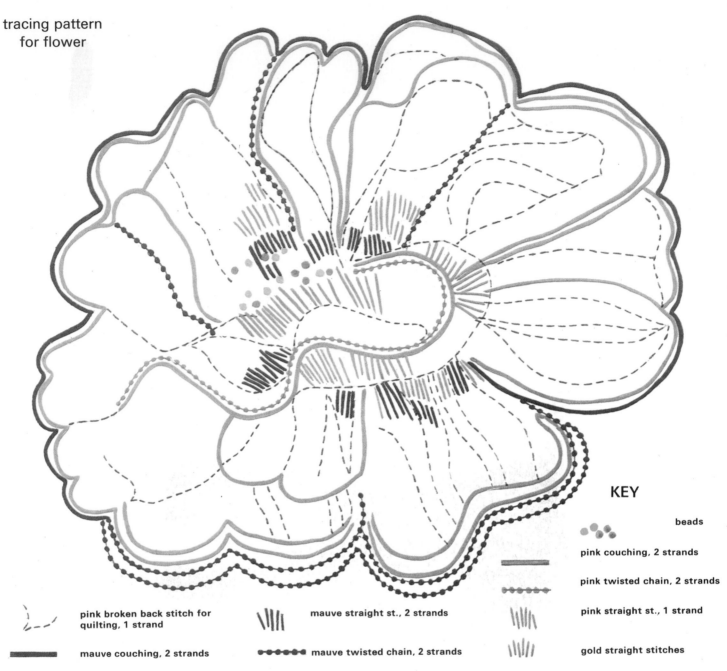

KEY

pink broken back stitch for
quilting, 1 strand

mauve couching, 2 strands

|||| mauve straight st., 2 strands

●●●●●●● mauve twisted chain, 2 strands

mauve floss.
The French knots can be placed anywhere, providing they heighten the
sense of flow and are used in groups of
one color. Use pearl cotton No. 5 and,
if desired, combine the stitchery with
beads. Work the green knots in a solid
mass as they touch the flower to add
depth and accentuate the three-
dimensional quality of the flower.

Using a frame
This panel would be best worked on a
frame, ideally one made specifically for
this piece (such as artists' canvas
stretchers). In that case, it need not be
removed after working.
Alternatively, remove the embroidery
from the working frame, stretch it over
hardboard and frame it.

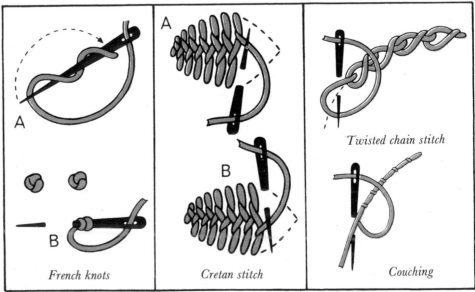

French knots   *Cretan stitch*   *Twisted chain stitch*

Couching

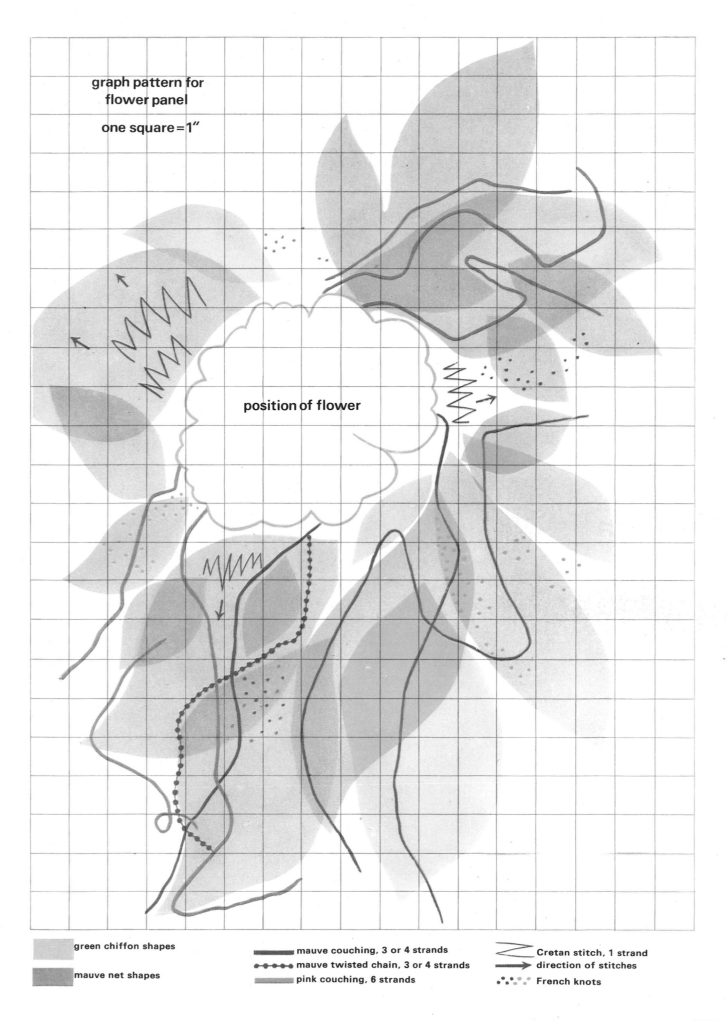

graph pattern for
flower panel

one square = 1"

position of flower

green chiffon shapes

mauve net shapes

mauve couching, 3 or 4 strands

mauve twisted chain, 3 or 4 strands

pink couching, 6 strands

Cretan stitch, 1 strand

direction of stitches

French knots

Dazzling diamonds

This brilliant long-line sweater in a kaleidoscope of colors is deceptively easy to make. It has been cleverly designed so that you never have to work with more than two colors at a time. It can be worn by itself or as a slipover, and should prove a useful garment.

Sizes
Directions are for 32in bust The sizes in brackets [ ] refer to the 34 and 36in bust sizes respectively
Length at side seams, 18[18:18]

Gauge
8 sts and 9 rows to 1in on No.2 needles

Materials
3-ply fingering yarn
1 oz, balls
2 [3:3] balls main color, Brown, A
1 ball each of 6 contrast colors, B, Pink;
C, Dark Red; D, Bright Red;
E, Yellow; F, Gray;
G, Blue
No. 1 knitting needles (or Canadian No. 12)
No. 2 knitting needles (or Canadian No. 11)

Back

Using No.1 needles and A, cast on 130[138:146] sts.
Work 43 rows K1, P1 rib.
44th row Dec one st at end of row, still working in rib. 129[137:145] sts.
Change to No.2 needles and st st. Attach and break off colors as required.
1st patt row Using B, K.
2nd patt row Using B, P.
3rd patt row K1 C, *K7 B, K1 C, rep from * to end.
4th patt row P1 C, *P7 B, P1 C, rep from * to end.

5th patt row K2 C, *K5 B, K3 C, rep from *, ending last rep K2 C.
6th patt row P2 C, *P5 B, P3 C, rep from *, ending last rep P2 C.
7th patt row K3 C, *K3 B, K5 C, rep from *, ending last rep K3 C.
8th patt row P3 C, *P3 B, P5 C, rep from *, ending last rep P3 C.
9th patt row K4 C, *K1 B, K7 C, rep from *, ending last rep K4 C.
10th patt row P4 C, *P1 B, P7 C, rep from *, ending last rep P4 C.
11th patt row Using C, K.
12th patt row Using C, P.
13th patt row K4 C, *K1 D, K7 C, rep from *, ending last rep K4 C.
14th patt row P4 C, *P1 D, P7 C, rep from *, ending last rep P4 C.
15th patt row K3 C, *K3 D, K5 C, rep from *, ending last rep K3 C.
16th patt row P3 C, *P3 D, P5 C, rep from *, ending last rep P3 C.
17th patt row K2 C, *K5 D, K3 C, rep from *, ending last rep K2 C.
18th patt row P2 C, *P5 D, P3 C, rep from *, ending last rep P2 C.
19th patt row K1 C, *K5 D, K3 C, rep from * to end.
20th patt row P1 C, *P5 D, P3 C, rep from * to end.
These 20 rows form the diamond patt and are continued throughout working the colors B, C, D, E, F, G, A in sequence, *at the same time*, dec one st at each end of next and every following 6th row, 8 times in all. 113[121:129] sts.
Continue without shaping for 17 rows more, working in the color patt.
Inc one st at each end of next and every following 10th row, 4 times in all. 121[129:137] sts.**
Continue without shaping for 9 rows more.

Shape armholes
Dec one st at each end of next and every other row until 61[65:69] sts rem.
Last row K.
Bind off.

Chart showing the color repeat

Front

Work as given for Back to **.
Continue without shaping for 8 rows more, working in color patt.

Divide for neck
Next row Patt 60[64:68] sts and slip on holder, P1 and leave this st on a safety pin, patt to end of row.
Continue on rem 60[64:68] sts for first shoulder.

Shape neck and armhole
Continue in patt, dec one st at each end of next and every other row 28[30:32] times.
Fasten off rem 2 sts tog.
Attach yarn to sts on holder and complete second shoulder to correspond.

Neckband

Using No.1 needles and A, cast on 48 sts for left shoulder strap, then onto same needle with RS facing, pick up and K 60[64:68] sts from left front neck edge, K st on safety pin, pick up and K 60[64:68] sts from right front neck edge, turn, cast on 48 sts for right shoulder strap, turn, pick up and K 61[65:69] sts from back neck edge. 278[290:302] sts.
1st row *K1, P1, rep from * to end.
2nd row Rib to within 2 sts of center front st, K2 tog tbl, K1, K2 tog, rib to end.
3rd row Rib to within 2 sts of center front st, P2 tog tbl, P center st, P2 tog.
Rep 2nd and 3rd rows once more, then 2nd row once.
Cast off in rib, working 2 sts tog at either side of center front st.

Armbands

Join row end edge of neckband.
Using No.1 needles and A, with RS facing, pick up and K 168[176:184] sts around armhole edge including shoulder strap.
Work 1 row K1, P1 rib.
Continue in rib, dec one st at each end of next 4 rows.
Cast off loosely in rib.

Finishing

Press all pieces under a damp cloth, using a warm iron, omitting ribbing.
Join side seams. Press.

2061

Handy hold-all

A large bag to hold odds and ends is a must for picnics, the beach, sports or swimming. This one is quick and easy to make, is very capacious and yet is smart enough to use on less informal occasions. The lining is detachable for easy washing.

Size
15in wide by 13in deep, excluding handles
Gusset depth, 3in

Gauge
4½sc and 5 rows to 1in worked on No. G hook
Each motif measures 3in across

Materials
Knitting Worsted
16 ounces
One No. F (4.00 mm) crochet hook
One No. G. (4.50 mm) crochet hook
4 one-inch curtain rings
2 pieces wood each 14 in. by ¾ in. by ¼ in.
1 yard iron-on ¾ in. wide tape
12 snap fasteners
⅝ yard 36 in. wide fabric
Piece buckram 1 yd. by 3 in.

Bag

1st motif
Using No.F hook, ch8. Join with ss to form a ring.
1st round Ch3, work 22dc into ring, join with ss to 3rd of ch3.
2nd round Ch8, skip 2dc, 1sc into next dc, ch4, skip 2dc, *1sc into next dc, ch6, skip 2dc, 1sc into next dc, ch4, skip 2dc, rep from * 3 times more, join with ss to 2nd of ch8. 8 loops.
3rd round *Into ch6 loop work 1sc, ch1, 6dc, ch1 and 1sc, into ch4 loop work 1sc, ch1, 2dc, ch1 and 1sc, rep from * 3 times more, join

with ss to first sc.
Fasten off.

2nd motif
Using No.F hook, ch8. Join with ss to form a ring.
1st and 2nd rounds As for first motif.
3rd round *Into ch6 loop work 1sc, ch1 and 3dc, join with ss between 3rd and 4th dc of any large petal on previous motif, into same ch6 loop work 3dc, ch1 and 1sc*, into ch4 loop work 1sc, ch1 and 1dc, join with ss between first and second dc of small petal, into same ch4 loop work 1dc, ch1 and 1sc, rep from * to * once more then complete as for first motif.
Work one row of five motifs in this manner.
Work a second row of motifs, working the second motif by joining on two sides by the method already given.
Continue in this manner until 4 rows of 5 motifs each have been completed.
Work the second side of the bag in the same manner.

Top edging
With RS facing, attach yarn to first motif on a 5 motif edge at center of large petal.
1st row *Ss into each of 4th, 5th and 6th dc of this petal, ch2, ss into each of 2dc of small petal, ch2, ss into each of first 3dc of large

petal, rep from * to end, turn. 60 sts.
2nd row Ch1, 1sc into each st to end.
Continue in sc for 12 rows more.
15th row 1tr into each st to end.
Fasten off.
Complete second side to correspond.

Gusset
Using No.G hook, ch14.
1st row 1sc into 3rd ch from hook, *1sc into next ch, rep from * to end. 13 sts.
Continue working in sc until work measures 38in.
Fasten off.

Handles
Using No.F hook, ch6.
1st row 1sc into 3rd ch from hook, *1sc into next ch, rep from * to end.
Continue working in sc until work measures 18in.
Fasten off.
Make a second handle in the same manner.

Rings
Using No.F hook and sc, crochet into each of the metal rings until completely covered.
Fasten off.

Finishing

On top edging fold to the

inside the row of tr and one row sc and stitch in place. This makes a channel for the pieces of wood.
With WS tog, position gusset with ends level with first row sc above motifs on top edging. Stitch, catching only the petal centers.
Cut out and sew lining, with ½in seam allowances. Fold over 2in on top edges. Position buckram on WS of gusset and stitch in position. Sew four snap fasteners at equal distances along each of the top edges of the lining and on the bag on 5th row sc above motifs.
Place another two snap fasteners at each top edge of the lining gusset and correspondingly on the bag gusset.
Iron tape onto WS of handles.
Loop 1½in at each end of handles through a ring and stitch in place. Attach rings to crochet top edging, positioning the lower edge of the ring on 2nd row sc.
Slot pieces of wood through top edging channels.
Place lining inside bag, WS tog and fasten with snaps.

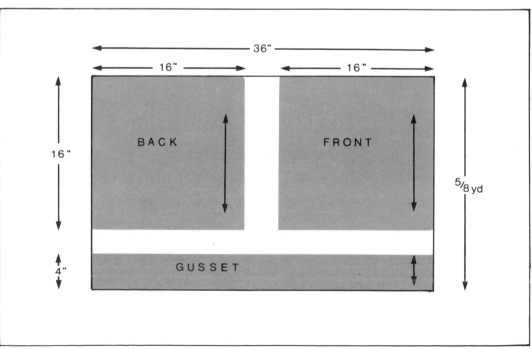

The layout of the pattern for the bag lining

2063

CRAFTS

Fireside slippers

Cozy, handmade slippers make individual and welcome presents. The techniques for making them are straightforward, and materials can be anything from left-over scraps of material to more elaborate velvets and sheepskins.

You will need:
- ☐ ¼ yard ¼ inch thick foam underlay, for inner soles
- ☐ ¼ yard 54 inch wide fur fabric, or sheepskin, for lining
- ☐ 1 yard 36 inch wide non-fray material, for uppers
- ☐ butt splits, leather or thin rubber, for soles
- ☐ strong button thread
- ☐ ⅛ yard Pellon or similar interlining, if material for uppers is lightweight
- ☐ latex adhesive
- ☐ pair of wedges, if required

To make slippers

To make a pair of flat slippers with plain toecaps, draw up the sole and toecap pieces from the graph. The sole and upper pieces given here are for small and medium slippers, with ½ inch seam allowance included throughout. Adjust both sole and upper pieces to give the size required. It is often worth making up the slippers first in cotton or canvas, so that the fit can be adjusted and the pattern pieces amended accordingly.

1. Cut out the inner soles from foam, taking care to reverse the pattern for cutting out the second sole. Cut out the lining in the same way. With wrong sides together and matching notches,

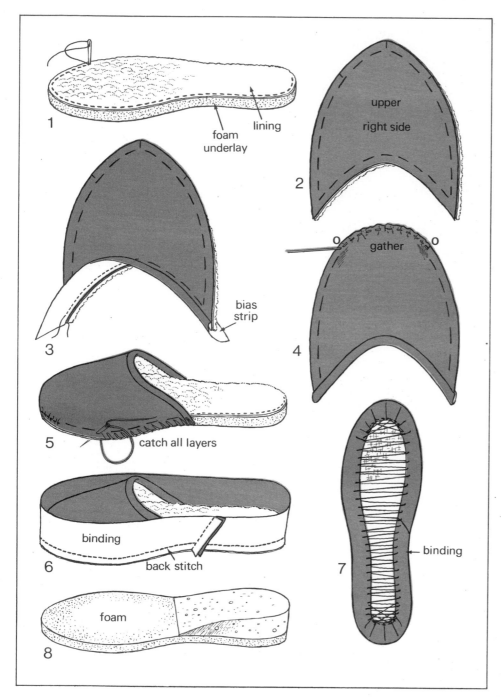

1

lining

foam
underlay

2

upper
right side

3

bias
strip

4

gather

5

catch all layers

6

binding

back stitch

7

binding

8

foam

Slippers with wedge soles

8. Cut out the inner sole as described in **1**. Glue the wedge to the inner sole as shown. Cut a second pair of inner soles and trim to fit the wedge. Glue to the first inner sole over the wedge, and stick the lining in position over the top. Follow steps **2**–**5** above.

To bind the sole, from the upper fabric cut one strip $1\frac{1}{2}$ inches deep and of sufficient length to bind the flat part of the sole, plus one inch. Cut a second strip long enough to cover the raised part of the sole plus one inch, with one long straight edge and one long edge $1\frac{1}{2}$ inches wide at either end and curving up to $2\frac{1}{2}$ inches in the center (or whatever measurement is the maximum depth of the wedge plus $1\frac{1}{2}$ inches). Stitch the short ends of the strip together to form a band, taking a $\frac{1}{2}$ inch seam allowance, and stitch the band to the sole as shown in **6**.

Finish off the slipper as previously described.

Variations of the basic slipper

The graph pattern gives alternative pattern pieces for slippers with a split toecap, or for slippers with a plain band instead of a toecap.

For slippers with a split toecap, draw up the pattern piece from the graph. The size given here is for a size 6 slipper. Cut two top pieces and two lining pieces for each slipper, taking care to reverse the pattern after cutting the first pieces.

With right sides together, join the upper pieces down the center of the toecap. Join the linings in the same way and stitch the uppers and the linings together, as described in **2**.

The advantage of this method is that the size of the toecap can easily be adjusted along the center seam to fit the foot. Apart from the central seam, the slipper is made up exactly as described in **1**–**7**.

For slippers with a band instead of a toecap, draw up the pattern piece from the graph and cut an upper, a lining and an interlining piece for each slipper.

From the upper fabric, cut also two bias strips for each slipper, each strip one inch deep and of sufficient length to bind the ankle or toe for each band. Make the slipper sole as described in **1** and **2**. Place the interlining to one side of the upper and stitch in position. Place the lining to the other side of the upper and stitch, leaving one side open for turning. Turn band to right side and slip stitch opening. Bind the edges of the band as described in **3**, and stitch to the sole as in **5**, matching notches 1–1 and 2–2 on sole.

Finish making up the slipper as described in **6** and **7**.

---

stitch the lining and inner sole together.

2. Cut out the uppers and linings. With wrong sides together and matching notches, baste and stitch around the upper and lining. If the upper material is fairly light, cut a toe shape from Pellon and stitch to the upper. Stitch the lining on the other side of the upper.

3. Cut a bias strip from the upper fabric, 1 inch wide and of sufficient length to bind the ankle edge of the upper. With right sides together, baste and stitch the bias strip to the ankle edge of the upper. Fold the bias strip over to the wrong side and slip stitch neatly in position. Turn under and neaten the raw edges of the bias strip.

4. Mark clearly the center point of the upper and gather the center front of the upper between the small circles with strong thread to form a block, as shown, matching ankle edges of toecap to notches 3–3 on sole.

5. With wrong sides together, stitch upper to sole, as shown.

6. From the upper fabric, cut a strip $1\frac{1}{2}$ inches wide and of sufficient length to bind right around the sole, plus one inch. Join the short ends of the strip to form a band, taking a $\frac{1}{2}$ inch seam allowance. Stitch the binding to the slipper, as shown. Cut notches in the binding at toe and heel, to reduce bulk.

7. Turn the binding over to the underside of the sole and lace firmly from side to side along the length of the sole, as shown.

Cut soles from butt splits, leather or rubber and stick securely to the inner sole.

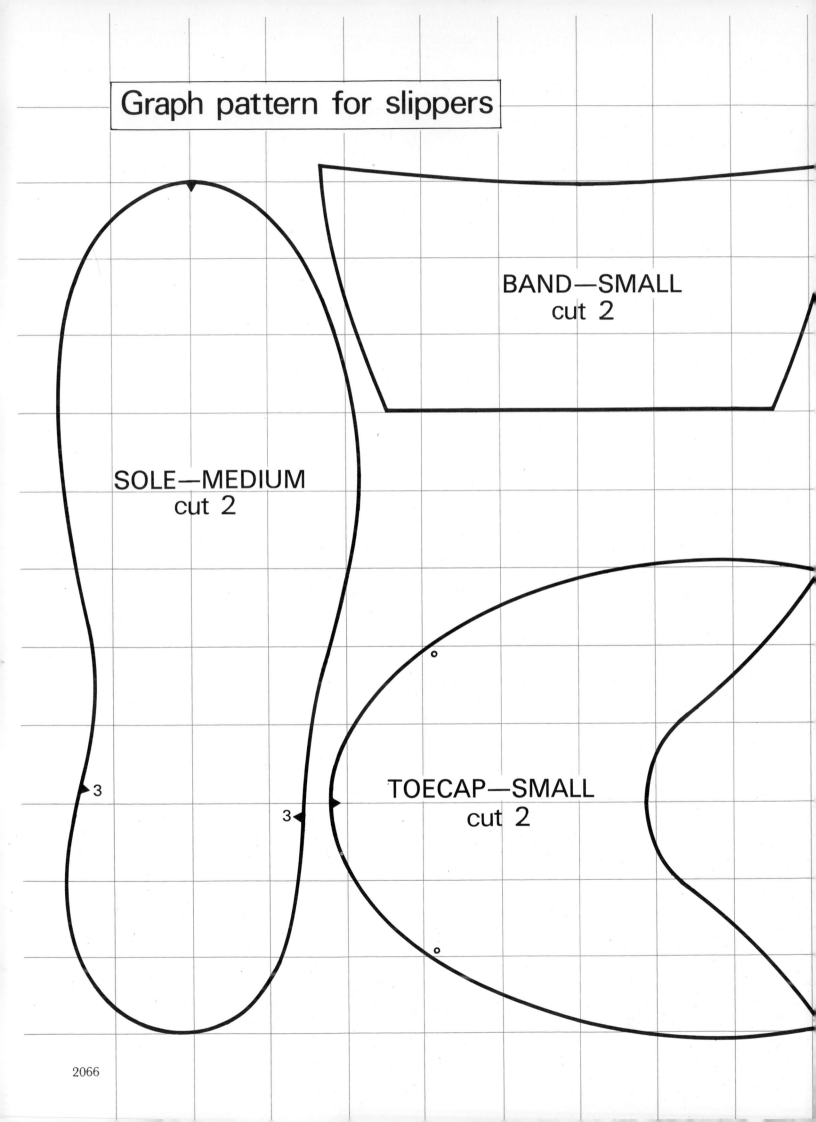

Graph pattern for slippers

BAND—SMALL
cut 2

SOLE—MEDIUM
cut 2

TOECAP—SMALL
cut 2

3

3

2066

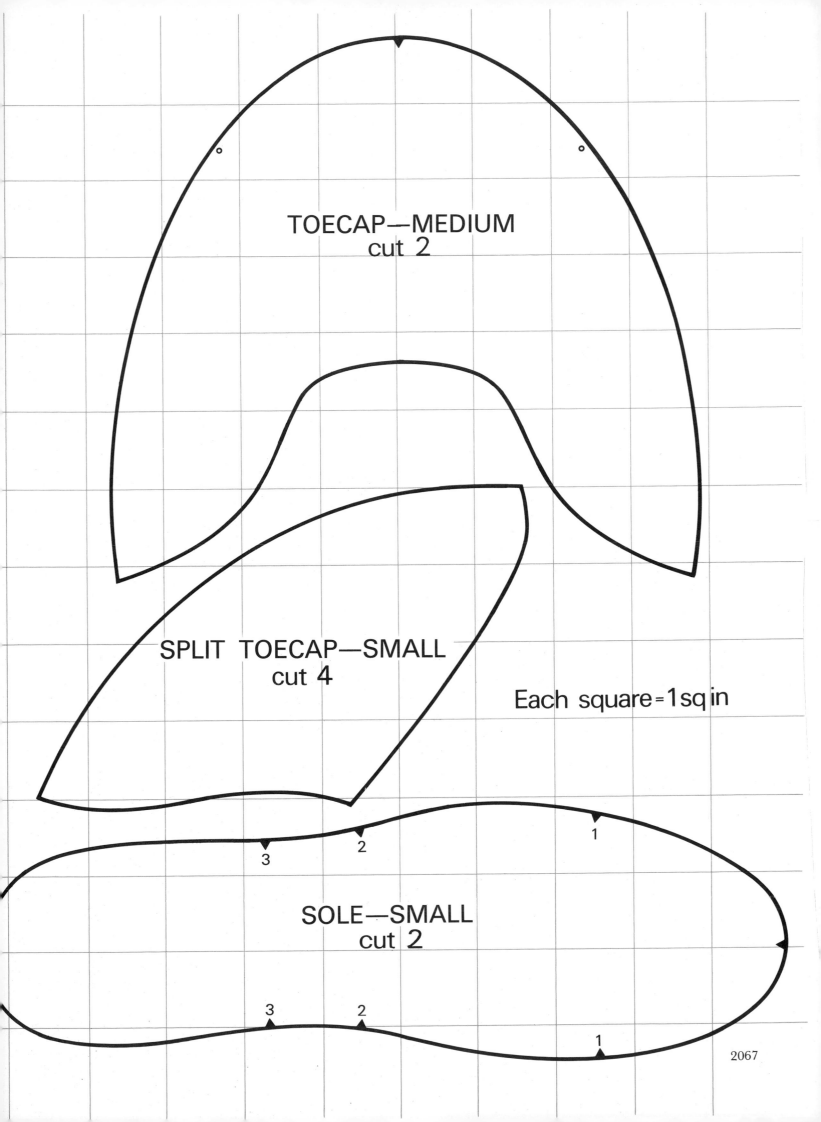

TOECAP—MEDIUM
cut 2

SPLIT TOECAP—SMALL
cut 4

Each square = 1 sq in

3   2   1

SOLE—SMALL
cut 2

3   2   1

2067

2068

Hanging gardens

A simple macramé braid can be used effectively to suspend plant pots or candle holders. These decorative pot covers can bring a touch of originality to a balcony or window.

Hanging bowl

Threads are set onto a curtain ring which is taped to the center of the base of the bowl. The shape is then enclosed in a pattern of alternate square knots.

Cut an even number of lengths of string each four times the depth of the container, plus five times the length of the suspension cords.

Set the doubled threads onto the ring. Turn the container upside down and tape the ring and threads to the center of the base.

Take each pair of double threads and tape to the bowl at the edge of the base. Make two square knots.

Using two threads from each square knot together with two threads from the next square knot, make two more square knots which will therefore be alternated with the first sets of knots.

Continue in alternated square knots to the rim of the bowl, taping the knots to keep them in place. Once the bowl is suspended, the knots will stay in place automatically and the tape can be removed.

Divide the threads as before and with each pair of doubled threads, work eight square knots. Thread a glass bead onto the two core threads, work twenty-one square knots, *thread on two small beads, work two square knots, repeat from * twice more, then work five square knots. Make an overhand knot with all four threads.

Taking all the suspension threads together, make a large overhand knot positioned ten inches from the last square knots.

For the bowl illustrated you will need:

Polished macramé twine
1 curtain ring
roll masking tape
5 rectangular glass beads
30 round beads

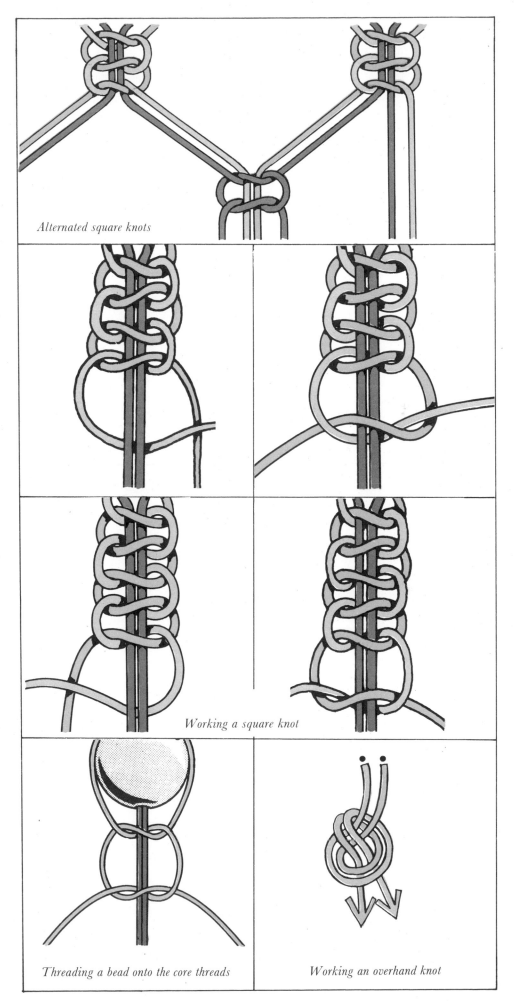

Alternated square knots

Working a square knot

Threading a bead onto the core threads

Working an overhand knot

Measurements
To fit bowl 4in deep, 8in diameter.
Length of suspension cords, 21in.

Method
On the bowl illustrated there are ten
lengths of twine, each ten feet long.

Large candle jar

The threads are set onto a curtain ring
which is taped to the center of the jar
base. The shape is then enclosed in a
pattern of square knots and beads. Cut
a number of lengths of string divisible
by eight, each ten times the depth of the
container and the diameter added together, plus ten times the length of the
suspension cord.
Set the doubled threads onto the ring in
groups of four doubled threads. Tape
the ring to the base. Tape each group of
threads to the edge of the base.
Divide the threads into two groups of
four threads each and work five square
knots on each group. Thread an oval
bead on the core threads of each group
and make one square knot to hold in
place. Using all eight threads together of
each group, make a square knot with
three threads on each side and two core
threads. Thread a round bead onto the
core threads of each group and make one
square knot to secure.
Divide each group into two groups of
four threads, make one square knot on
each group, pass core threads through an
oval bead, then make five square knots.
Tape the completed braids in place.
Take each group of four threads to slope
toward the group of four in the next
group, to alternate the groupings.
With each new group of eight threads *
make a square knot with three threads on
either side of two core threads, pass the
core threads through a small round bead,
make another square knot to secure *.
Divide the threads into groups of four
and work five square knots on each
group, thread an oval bead onto the core
threads, make one square knot to secure.
Alternate the groups to take them back
to their original grouping, repeat from
* to within one inch of the top of the jar.
Tape groups in place.
Cut four lengths of thread each ten times
the circumference of the top of the jar.
Double and set onto a short holding cord.
Work from * to * until braid fits jar top
tightly.
Pass the ends through the set-on threads
at the beginning to make a circle and
knot in pairs at the back of the work.
Trim ends and glue.
Position this band around the top of the
jar, over the threads already worked.
Lightly glue in place.

Continue on the original groups of eight
threads. Using four core threads and two
threads on each side, work twenty-three
square knots. Make an overhand knot
with each pair of side threads and trim.
Using the four remaining threads, work
one square knot, thread a round bead
onto center two threads, then work
twenty-three square knots.
Taking all the threads together from the
four groups, make one large overhand
knot. Trim tassel.

For the jar illustrated you will need:
Cotton seine macramé twine
1 curtain ring
32 small round beads
12 oval wooden beads
masking tape
candle

Measurements
To fit jar 7½in deep, 3in diameter.
Length of suspension cords, 10in.

Method
On the jar illustrated there are sixteen
lengths each sixteen feet long.
The two opposite groups have orange
oval beads and the alternate opposite
groups have yellow oval beads.
The repeat from * was worked once only
to * to reach within one inch of the jar
top.
For the band around the top of the jar,
from * to * was worked sixteen times.

Hanging plant pot

The threads are set onto a curtain ring
which is placed inside the pot and the
threads are taken through the hole in
the base to the outside. The shape is then
enclosed in a pattern of alternated
square knots.
Cut an even number of threads each four
times the depth of the pot plus five times
the length of the suspension cords.
Insert the ring inside the pot and draw
the threads through the hole to the
outside.
Work square knots on each group of four
threads until the edge of the base is
reached. Tape in place.
Divide the threads into pairs and taking
one pair from one group together with a
pair from the next group, work two
square knots on each group. Tape the
knots in place.
Again taking two threads from one
group together with two threads from the
next group, work two square knots on
each group.
Continue in this way, alternating the
position of the knots, and work to the
top of the pot.
With each group, work eight square

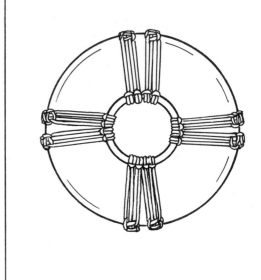

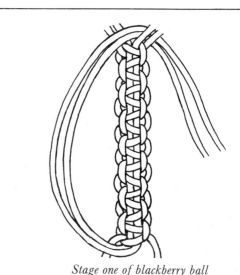

Stage one of blackberry ball

knots. Using a blunt-ended needle,
thread the two central threads from front
to back through the work above the
center of the first knot. Pull up until a
little blackberry-shaped roll is formed.
Make two square knots to secure.
Using the first two stages of the square
knot only so that the braid twists, continue until spiral measures four inches.
Pass all the threads of each group through
a large glass bead.
Continue in half knots but using the
previous core threads as outside threads
and vice versa. Work another four inches
of spiral braid. Make an overhand knot
on each group.
Taking all threads from the four groups
together, make a large overhand knot
seven inches above the small overhand
knots. Trim the tassel.

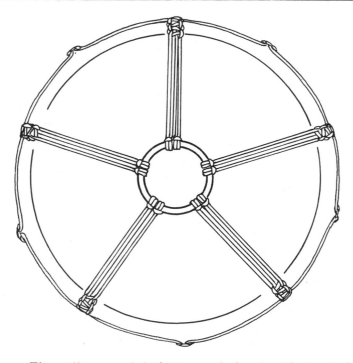
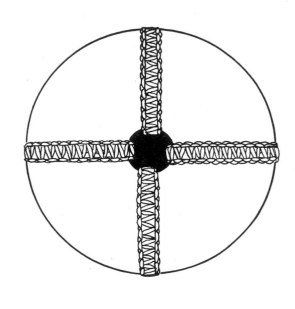

The cording around the bottom of the large candle jar, the hanging bowl and plant pot

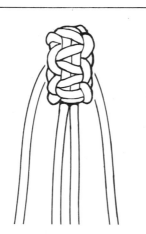

The ball pulled up tight

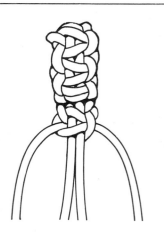

The securing square knot below

Working the spiral

Knotting single thread left

For the pot illustrated you will need:
soft white cord
1 curtain ring
masking tape
4 large rectangular glass beads

Measurements
To fit pot 5½in deep, 6in top diameter.
Length of suspension cords, 18in.

Method
On the pot illustrated there are eight threads, each ten feet long.

Jar with lip

The jar is held just under the lip by one braid of single knotted chain and hung from three suspension cords.

Cut one length of twine eight times the circumference of the jar, and two lengths each five times the length of the suspension cords.

Using the long piece of twine, fold it in half and pin to a secure base. Using the right-hand thread as core, knot the left-hand thread around it once, leaving a small loop at the top, then using the left-hand thread as core, knot the right-hand thread around it. This is called single knotted chain. Continue in this way for the circumference of the jar less one inch. Fit the braid around the jar, pass the ends of the string through the loop at the beginning and pull the braid up so that it is tight.

Continue in single knotted chain until a further twelve inches have been worked. Using a crochet hook, pull each of the

other two lengths through the knotted chain around the jar, one on each side of the first suspension chain, a third of the way around the jar. Pull the ends even and work single knotted chain for twelve inches.

Taking all six threads together, make one large overhand knot. Trim ends.

For the jar illustrated you will need:
Polished macramé twine
One crochet hook

Measurements
To fit jar 4½in deep
Length of suspension cords, 12in

Method
For the jar illustrated there are one six foot length and two five foot lengths.

GENTLE ARTS

Embroidery on tulle

Embroidery on tulle gives a fine, delicate effect ideal for handkerchief edgings. This very special handkerchief would make a charming gift.

Materials you will need
- ☐ ½yd tulle
- ☐ ⅓yd lawn
- ☐ 1 skein D.M.C. Coton à Broder No.16
- ☐ thin cardboard or stiff paper
- ☐ basting thread

Preparing the pattern
Trace the outline pattern, including the guide lines. The corner section can either be repeated all around to give the full edging pattern or it can be worked from the one section, moving the pattern around as each corner is completed. Transfer the design to colored cardboard or stiff paper, so that the white meshes of the tulle will show more clearly.

Working on tulle
Because of its transparent quality, embroidery on tulle has to be as neat on the back as on the front. When beginning, work two or three running stitches in the wrong direction and then double back over these to secure. To finish off, darn back into the work with several running stitches and trim the end close to the fabric.

Preparing the fabric
Work in running stitch along a line of meshes to find the straight of the fabric, and then again along another line of meshes at right angles to the first one. Position these threads against the outer guide lines of one corner and.pin the fabric in place. Work running stitch along the remaining outer and inner edge lines.
Baste the tulle to the pattern all around and trim the fabric, leaving an allowance of about one inch all around.

Applying the center
Place a square of cotton lawn under the center of the tulle, leaving an allowance of about one inch all around the inner guide line. Baste in position. Work in double buttonhole stitch over the run-

ning stitch thread, through the double thickness of tulle and lawn.
Using a fine pair of manicure scissors, trim away the tulle on the inner edge and the lawn on the outer edge.

The stitches

Running stitch
Pass the needle over one mesh of the tulle and under the next, alternately.

Ring filling
Follow the line of the curve in running stitch. As each ring is reached, working in a counter-clockwise direction outline one mesh hole in running stitch.

Spot filling
Work a thread in running stitch around one mesh hole and then work buttonhole stitch over it to form a ring.

Cording
First work a running stitch up the stem, then work three small overcast stitches each into a different mesh and each time returning to the stem mesh for each

petal and then overcast the running stitch.

Buttonhole stitch edging
Embroider over the running stitch guide, working one buttonhole stitch for each mesh of tulle.

Double buttonhole stitch edging
Work in buttonhole stitch over the running stitch, then work a second row of buttonhole stitch in the opposite direction, interlocking it with the first row.

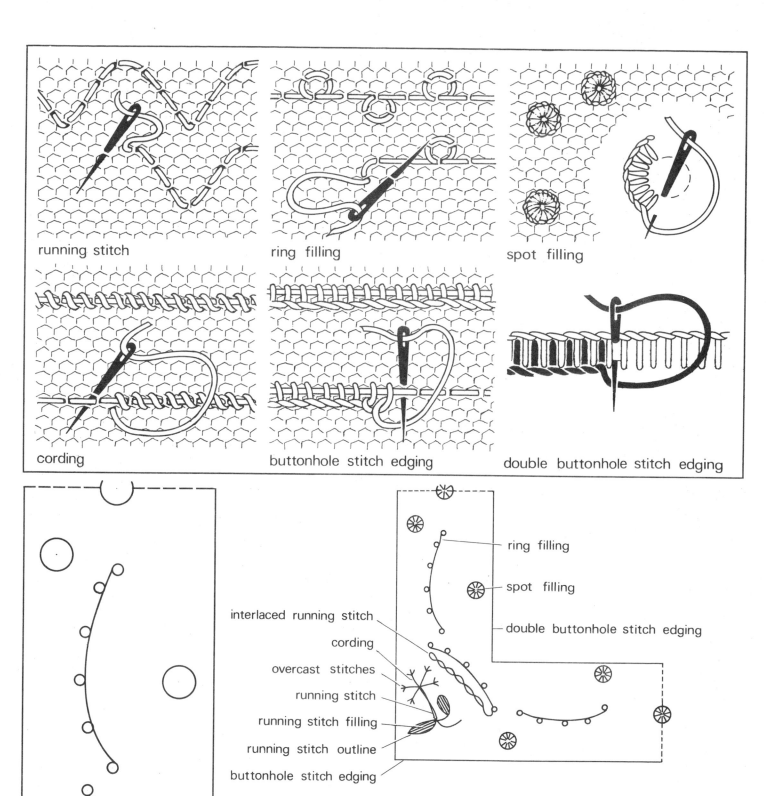

running stitch

ring filling

spot filling

cording

buttonhole stitch edging

double buttonhole stitch edging

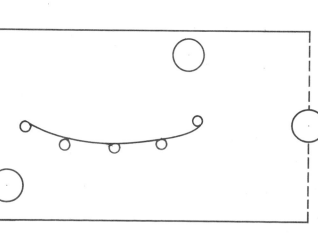

ring filling

spot filling

double buttonhole stitch edging

interlaced running stitch

cording

overcast stitches

running stitch

running stitch filling

running stitch outline

buttonhole stitch edging

Tracing pattern
for border

2073

2074

QUICK MAKE

The demure look

This romantic, hooded dress has a close-fitting yoke and cuffs boldly embroidered with large roses. Details of how to work the embroidery are given in Stitchery Ideas on page 2079. If the embroidery is to be worked, it should be completed on the appropriate pieces before making the garment. The dress could be left plain, or made with a contrasting fabric for the yoke and cuffs. If desired, the pattern could also be extended to make a full-length dress.

Fabrics and notions

For this hooded dress (excluding embroidery materials) you will need:
- $5\frac{1}{4}$ yards 36 inch wide fabric such as Viyella or nun's veiling ($6\frac{1}{4}$ yards if the dress is to be full length)
- $\frac{1}{4}$ yard 36 inch wide woven interfacing for cuffs
- sewing thread to match fabric
- 13 dome or ball buttons
- graph paper for pattern

The pattern

The pattern given here is for sizes 10, 12, 14 and 16.

Using the graph paper, draw up each pattern piece to scale. No seam allowances are included on the pattern so add $\frac{5}{8}$ inch to all edges and $1\frac{1}{2}$ inches on the skirt hem when cutting out the pattern pieces.

To make the dress

1. With right sides together, matching notches, baste and stitch the front yokes to the back yoke at the shoulder seams.

2. With right sides together, matching notches, baste and stitch the center back seam of the hood. Press the seams open and notch the curved seam allowance where necessary.

3. With right sides together, matching notches to shoulder seams and center backs, baste and stitch the hood to the neckline of the yoke. Repeat the process for the yoke and hood facing.

4. With right sides together, baste and stitch the hood and yoke to the hood and yoke facing at center front of yoke and around the front edge of the hood. Turn the hood and yoke to the right side and

baste around the seamed edge, easing it into shape and press. Run a double line of gathering stitches along the top of the skirt back and front.

5. With right sides together, baste and stitch the back skirt to the back yoke, drawing up the gathers evenly to fit and leaving free the back yoke facing.

6. Reinforce the center front of the skirt and slash to the stitching line as shown. With right sides together, baste and stitch the front skirt to the front yokes, matching the center front of yokes to the center front of skirt and drawing up the gathers evenly to fit, leaving free

the yoke facings.

Press the seams toward the shoulders. With right sides together, matching notches, baste and stitch the skirt side seams. Press the seams open.

Catch stitch the neckline seam on the yoke and yoke facing together by hand. Turn the raw edges on the front and back yokes and stitch by hand to the row of machine stitching.

7. Baste the yoke and yoke facing together around the armholes.

8. Reinforce the lower edge of the sleeve by machine stitching along the dotted line indicated on the pattern.

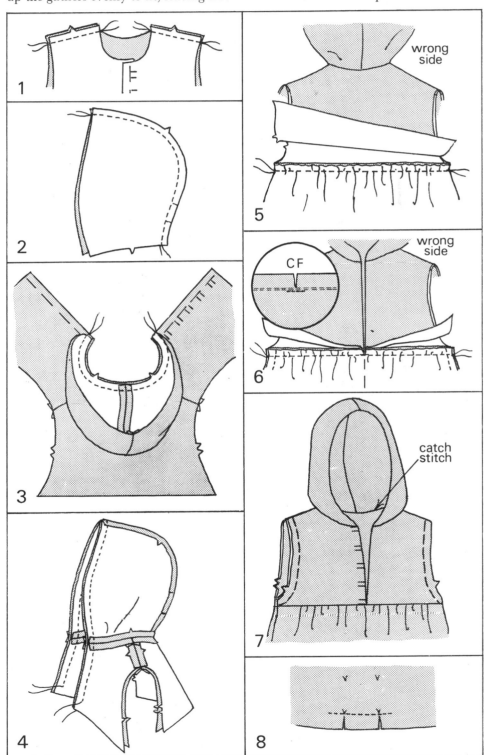

9. Clip the notches to the stitching line. Finish the lower edge between the clips with a narrow hand-turned hem. With right sides together, baste and stitch the sleeve seams. Press the seams open.

Run a double line of gathering stitches around the lower edge of the sleeve.

Baste the interfacing to the wrong side of the cuff and catch stitch loosely at the fold line.

10. With right sides together, pin the cuff to the sleeve, drawing up the sleeve gathers evenly to fit. Baste and stitch. Trim the interfacing close to the stitching. Layer the seam allowances. Press the seam toward the cuff.

Fold the cuff on the fold line with right sides together and stitch the ends. Trim the seams.

11. Turn the cuff to the right side. Slip stitch the free edge over the seam.

12. With right sides together, matching underarm seams, notches and the large circle to the shoulder seam, pin the sleeve into the armhole, easing out the fullness evenly. Stitch with the sleeve uppermost. Press the seam allowances together toward the sleeve.

Turn up the hem of the skirt to the required depth and sew with invisible hem stitch.

Work buttonhole loops down the front yoke and on the sleeve cuffs as indicated on the pattern. Sew buttons in position to match the loops.

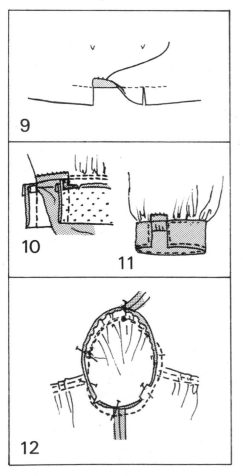

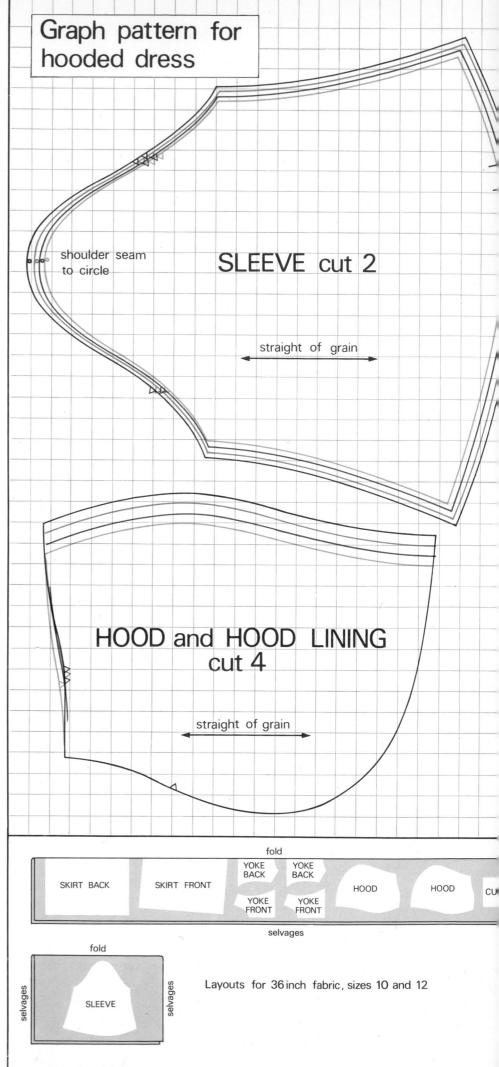

Graph pattern for hooded dress

shoulder seam to circle

SLEEVE cut 2

straight of grain

HOOD and HOOD LINING cut 4

straight of grain

fold

| SKIRT BACK | SKIRT FRONT | YOKE BACK | YOKE BACK | HOOD | HOOD | CU |

YOKE FRONT | YOKE FRONT

selvages

fold

selvages   SLEEVE   selvages

Layouts for 36 inch fabric, sizes 10 and 12

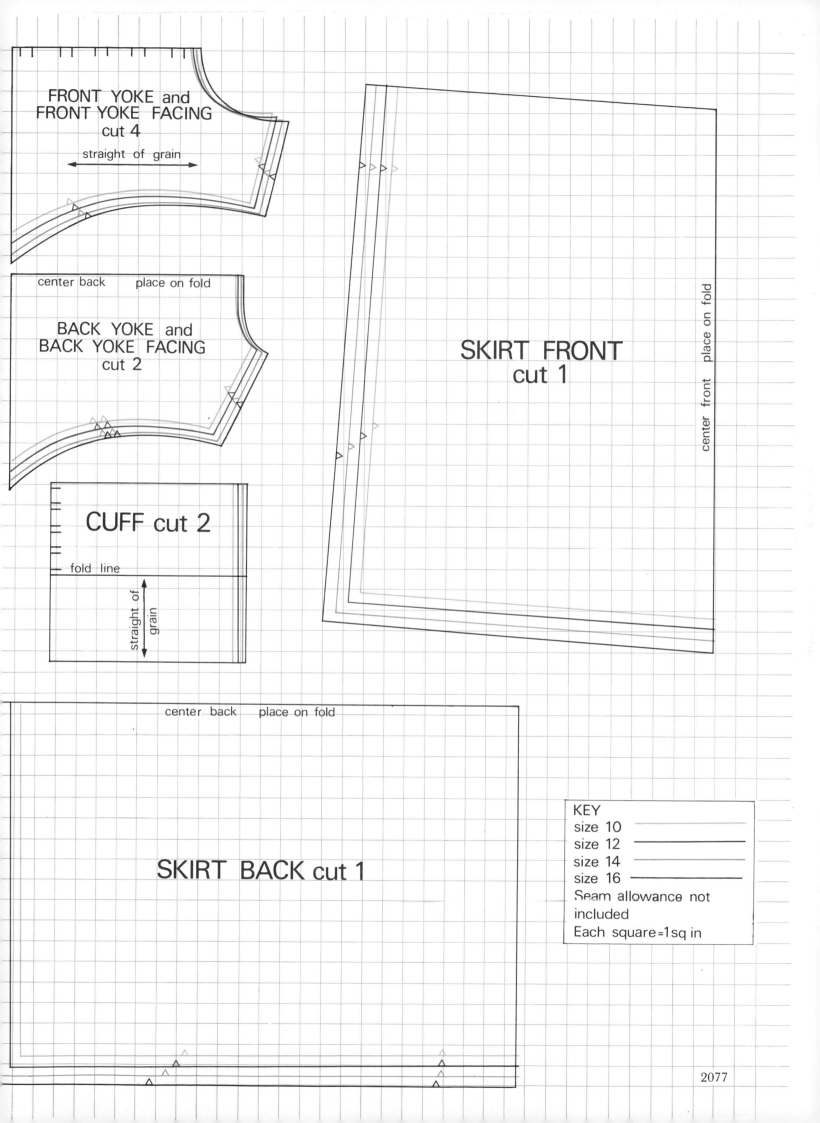

FRONT YOKE and
FRONT YOKE FACING
cut 4

straight of grain

center back   place on fold

BACK YOKE and
BACK YOKE FACING
cut 2

CUFF cut 2

fold line

straight of grain

SKIRT FRONT
cut 1

center front   place on fold

center back   place on fold

SKIRT BACK cut 1

KEY
size 10
size 12
size 14
size 16
Seam allowance not
included
Each square=1sq in

2077

Tracing pattern for the embroidery

D.M.C. 6-Strand Floss

962
rose pink

899
carnation

906
parrot green

Layout shows placement of motifs on yoke

Long and short stitch

2078

The romance of roses

These vivid roses are bold, pretty embroidery motifs which may be worked entirely in long and short stitch. Illustrated on the hooded dress on page 2074, they look just as suitable worked on household linens.

To work the embroidery

Materials required
☐ D.M.C. 6-Strand floss in the following colors and quantities:
    3 skeins 962 rose pink
    2 skeins 899 carnation
    3 skeins 906 parrot green
☐ No. 5 embroidery needle

Placing the motifs
For the embroidery on the yoke, use the motifs once as shown in the tracing pattern and once reversed as a mirror image for the second yoke piece. Use an alternating mirror image of the small rose motifs, working three on each cuff.

Method of working
After tracing the motifs onto the two yoke pieces and cuffs, work the embroidery in long and short stitch, using three strands of floss in the needle. This should be done before making up the dress.

Adapting the motifs

As a pleasing alternative, group four of the large motifs in the center of a small linen tablecloth. Place one small motif in the corner of each of a set of matching napkins. Gold and orange on a background of beige linen would be a warm combination, perhaps with olive-green leaves.
Or work a row of the smaller roses on a strip of fabric to be used as curtain tie-backs, using the same fabric as the curtains. The result is particularly gay if the fabric is dotted or striped.
Another idea is to work the roses in appliqué on a bedspread, using scraps of cotton fabric (try combining solid colors and prints, as in patchwork). Individual petals and leaves can be stitched to the background fabric either by hand or machine.

Large and small roses are versatile embroidery motifs, used either singly or in groups

2079

Pretty cover-up

Here is a pretty hostess apron which has been designed to look feminine and attractive and still give maximum coverage in the kitchen. The main section is worked in an interesting new stitch.

Size
Directions are for 24–26in waist adjustable
Length from shoulder to hem, 38in

Gauge
6 sc and 5 rows to 1in worked on No. E hook

Materials
Coats & Clark's O.N.T. Speed Cro-Sheen, 10 (100 yd.) balls
One No. E (3.50 mm) crochet hook
2 buttons

Apron

Using No.E hook, ch49.
1st row Insert hook into 2nd ch from hook, yrh and draw through, yrh and draw through one loop, yrh and draw through 2 loops – called 1ssc (single single crochet) – 1ssc into each ch to end, turn. 48 sts.
2nd row Ch2, skip first ssc, 1ssc into each of next 9ssc, 2ssc into next ssc, 1ssc into each ssc to last 11ssc, 2ssc into next ssc, 1ssc into each ssc to end, 1ssc into 2nd of ch2, turn.
3rd row Ch2, skip first ssc, *1ssc into next ssc, rep from * to end, 1ssc into 2nd of ch2, turn.
Rep last row 4 times more, then 2nd row once.

2080

Continue in this manner, inc on every 6th row until there are 80 sts.
Fasten off.

Edging

1st row With RS facing, attach yarn to side edge at waist and work 96ssc into row ends down edge of apron, 2ssc at corner, 84ssc along lower edge, 2ssc at corner and 96ssc up other edge, turn.

2nd row Ch4, *skip 1ssc, 1dc into next ssc, ch1, rep from * to corner, (1dc, ch2) twice into corner sp, 1dc into same sp, ch1, rep from * along lower edge, work corner as before, rep from * up second side edge ending with 1dc into last ssc, turn.

3rd row Ch4, (1tr into first dc, ch2, ss into top of tr – called 1 picot –) 4 times, *ch2, skip 2 sps, 1sc into next sp, ch2, skip 2 sps, (1tr, 1 picot) 7 times into next sp, rep from * 6 times more, ch2, skip 2 sps, 1sc into next sp, ch2, skip 2 sps, (1tr, 1 picot) 3 times into each of next 4 sps, beg at * work along lower edge and other side edge in the same manner, working second corner as before and ending with ch2, skip 2 sps, 1sc into next sp, ch2, skip 2sps, (1tr, 1 picot) 4 times into 3rd of ch4, 1tr into same place, turn.

4th row Ss to first picot, *ch3, 1sc into next picot, rep from * to end of first gr, 1sc into first picot of next gr, rep from * all around counting the 12 picots at each corner as one gr, and ending with ch3, 1sc into last picot, turn.

5th row Ch3, 1dc into last sc made, (ch3, keeping last loop of each st on hook work 3dc into next ch3 sp, yoh and draw through all loops on hook – called 1cl –) 3 times, *ch1, (1cl into next ch3 sp, ch3) 5 times, 1cl into next ch3 sp*, rep from * to * 6 times more, **ch1, (1cl into next ch3 sp, ch3) 10 times around corner, 1cl into next ch3 sp**, rep from * to * 6 times along lower edge, then from ** to ** around second corner, then from * to * up second side edge, ending with ch3, 2dc into first ss of 4th row, turn.

6th row (Ch3, 1cl into next ch3 sp) 3 times, *ch1, (1cl into next ch3 loop, ch3) 4 times, 1cl into next ch3 loop*, rep from * to * 6 times more, **ch1, (1cl into next ch3 loop, ch3) 9 times around corner, 1cl into next ch3 loop**, rep from * to * 6 times then from ** to ** once for second corner, then from * to * up second side edge, ending with ch1, (1cl into next ch3 loop, ch3) twice, 1cl into last ch3 loop, 1dc into 3rd of ch3, turn.

7th row *Ch4, 1sc into next ch3 sp, rep from * all around, ending with ch1, 1dc into 3rd of ch3, turn.

8th row 3sc into first ch4 loop, *(2sc, ch3, 1 picot into top of last sc worked, 2sc) into next ch4 loop, rep from * to last loop, 3sc into last loop.
Fasten off.

Waistband

Using No.E hook, ch59, without breaking off yarn and with RS facing, work 12 ssc into top of apron edging, 48ssc into top of apron skirt, 12ssc into top of second apron edging, ch60, turn.

2nd row 1sc into 2nd ch from hook, 1sc into each ch, 1sc into each ssc, 1sc into each ch, turn. 190sc.

3rd row Ch1, 1sc into each sc to end, turn.
Rep last row 3 times more.

Next row (buttonhole) 1sc into each of next 4sc, ch4, skip 4sc, 1sc into each of next 32 sc, ch4, skip 4sc, 1sc into each sc to end, turn.

Next row As 3rd but working 4sc into each ch4 loop.
Rep 3rd row 4 times more.
Fasten off.

Straps

Using No.E hook, ch25.
1st row As 1st row of apron. 24ssc.
2nd row As 3rd row of apron.

3rd row Ch1, 1ssc into each of next 9ssc, leaving last loop of each st on hook work 1ssc into each of the next 2 ssc, yoh and draw through all loops on hook – called dec 1 – turn.

4th row 1ssc into each st, turn.

5th row 1ssc into each st to within last 2 sts, dec 1, turn.
Rep last 2 rows until 8 sts rem.

Continue in ssc without shaping until strap measures 30in.
Fasten off.

Attach yarn to 13ssc on waistband, dec 1, 1ssc into each st to end, turn.
Work to correspond with first strap, reversing shapings.
Fasten off.

Edging

Attach yarn to outer edge of strap at waist.
Work 156sc along outer edge, turn.

Work rows 2 to 8 of apron edging, skipping shaping at corners and reading sc for ssc on 2nd row.
Fasten off.
Work edging on second strap in same manner.
Position straps centrally on waistband and stitch in place.

Button loops

Join yarn to end of strap on frill edge, work 10sc along frill edge, 8sc along end of strap, turn.

Next row Ch1, 1sc into each of 2sc, ch4, skip 4sc, 1sc into next 2sc, turn.

Next row Ch1, 1sc into each of next 2sc, 4sc into ch4 loop, 2sc into last 2sc.
Fasten off.

Finishing

Position buttons on waistband to correspond with buttonholes on other end of waistband and straps.
Press under a damp cloth using a warm iron.

Back view showing fastening

Dainty and feminine

Nothing could be simpler or more easy to make than this pretty nightgown in a delicate batiste fabric. Make it long or short and wear it for sleeping pretty.

Measurements

The instructions given here are for a nightgown to fit sizes 32 to 40 inch bust. The fitting is achieved by rows of casing ribbon threaded with elastic.

Requirements

- ☐ 3 yards 36 inch wide fabric
- ☐ 4¼ yards 1½ inch wide lace
- ☐ 11 yards ⅜ inch wide fine ribbon for casing and shoulder straps
- ☐ 5 yards hat elastic
- ☐ sewing thread to match fabric

To make the nightgown

Trim the fabric so that it is even at both ends. Fold and cut the fabric in half lengthwise.

With right sides together, baste and stitch the side seams. Press the seams open.

1. Working along the top edge of the fabric, turn and baste a ½ inch hem to the wrong side of the nightgown. Baste and stitch ribbon along the top to cover the raw edge of the hem, turning in the cut ends of the ribbon.

2. Stitch the lace trimming to the right side of the nightgown along the top edge.

3. Working from the top edge of the fabric and on the wrong side, measure and mark with tailor's chalk or pencil, four rows each spaced 3 inches apart as guide lines for placing the casing ribbon. Stitch four rows of casing ribbon to the wrong side, using the markings as a guide.

Cut the hat elastic into five equal lengths and, using a bodkin, thread a length through each casing. Draw up the elastic to fit and secure the ends firmly in a square knot. Trim off the excess elastic. Try on the nightgown and mark the hem length required, less the depth of the lace. Stitch the lace trimming to the right side along the marked line with a small, narrow zigzag stitch. Carefully trim the excess fabric close to the stitching.

4. Cut two shoulder straps from the ribbon and stitch them in position to the top of the nightgown. Catch the lace to the ribbon on each strap.

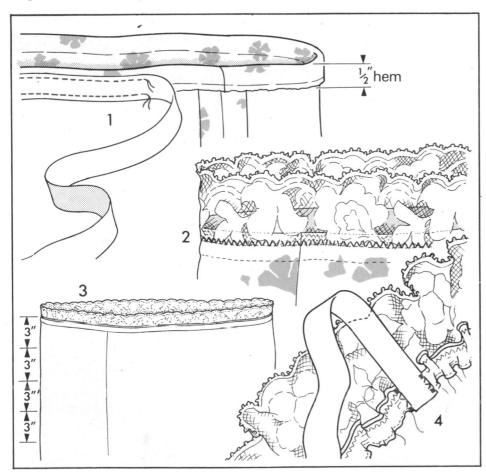

TOYS

Country cousin

Here is a really traditional rag doll to sew. Pretty as a picture with her pink cheeks and old-fashioned pinafore, she is simple to make and delightful to look at.

You will need:

For the body:
- ☐ 1 yard cream linen or muslin
- ☐ 1 bag of kapok
- ☐ 2 ounces sports yarn in brown-gold, for hair
- ☐ scraps of pink and gray felt, 6-strand floss, for features
- ☐ 1 foot black ribbon, for bow

For the clothes:
- ☐ 1½ yards flowered material, for dress
- ☐ 1½ yards plain cotton material, for pinafore and pantaloons
- ☐ 4 yards lace or braid
- ☐ shirring elastic
- ☐ 2 buttons
- ☐ 4 snap fasteners or hooks and eyes
- ☐ 1 square foot felt, for shoes' rosettes; beads or lace, for trimming

To make the doll

Draw up pattern pieces from the graph, in which one square equals one inch. A half inch seam allowance is included throughout. Cut two body pieces, four arm shapes and four legs. With right sides together, baste and stitch the body sections, leaving the top of the head open. Turn the body to the right side and stuff tightly. Slip stitch the head opening. Place two leg pieces right sides together, baste and stitch, leaving the top of the leg open. Turn to the right side and stuff tightly, making sure that the kapok is pushed well down into the toe. Stitch the leg securely to the base of the body, positioning leg seams at the front and back with the toe pointing forward. Repeat for the second leg. Stitch and stuff the arms in the same way, and sew securely in position at the shoulders.

Hair

Wind a 20-foot length of yarn into a skein of ten loops, each one foot long. This can be done most easily by winding the yarn ten times around the length of a 12-inch ruler.

Hold both ends of the skein together in one hand and with one finger of the other hand twist the loop until the yarn curls on itself. Fold the curled skein in half along its length, tuck the loose ends underneath, and stitch in position across the forehead to form curly bangs. Repeat to cover the top and back of the doll's head. Stitch further curled skeins around the sides and back of the head, leaving the lower ends free to form ringlets. Tie a bow of black ribbon and stitch at one temple.

Features

Cut two circles of pink felt $1\frac{1}{4}$ inches in diameter for cheeks and apply each to the face with two circles of chain stitch. Work the eye outlines in dark brown chain stitch. Cut two circles of gray felt each $\frac{1}{4}$ inch in diameter for eyes, and chain stitch in position. Work a few vertical stitches in dark brown thread in the center of each eye, to form pupils. To work the eyelashes, make a row of looped stitches along the upper and lower eyelid, securing the base of each loop with a small stitch. Cut through the loops. Work eyebrows in dark brown chain stitch. Work two cross-stitches in pink for nostrils, and a semicircle of pink chain stitch to form the chin. Work the outline of the mouth in red chain stitch, and fill in the lips with satin stitch.

Clothes

Shoes

Draw up the pattern pieces from the graph. Cut out the pieces from the felt square. Blanket stitch the side strip to the sole, and join the back seam with blanket stitch. Blanket stitch the toe of the shoe to the shoe side, and decorate the front with a small rosette, lace or beads. Slip the shoe onto the foot and secure with a few invisible stitches. Repeat for the second shoe.

Pantaloons

Draw up the pattern piece from the graph, and cut out the pieces from the plain fabric. With right sides together, stitch the side seams and inside leg seams and press flat. Turn to the right side and turn a narrow hem at waist and ankle edges. Gather waist to fit doll with shirring elastic, and gather ankle

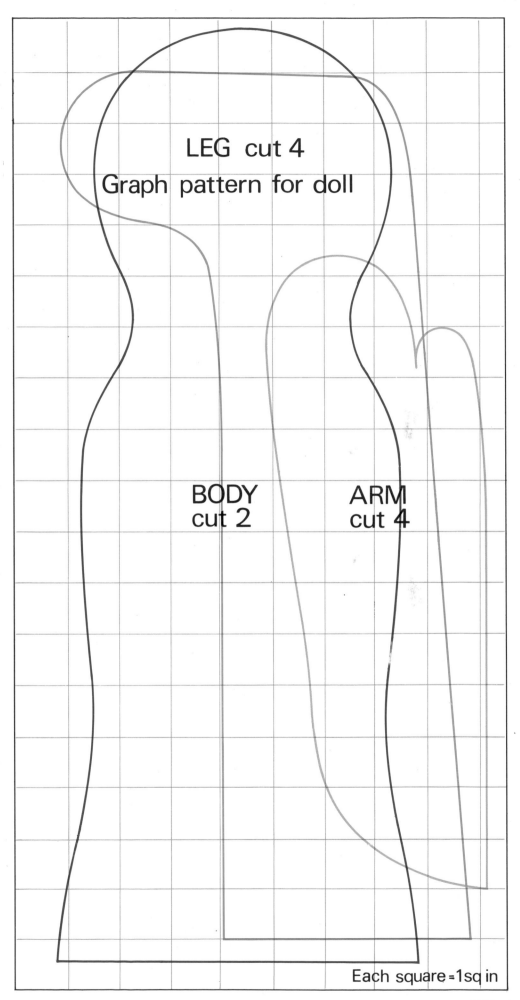

LEG cut 4
Graph pattern for doll

BODY
cut 2

ARM
cut 4

Each square = 1 sq in

Graph pattern for doll's clothes

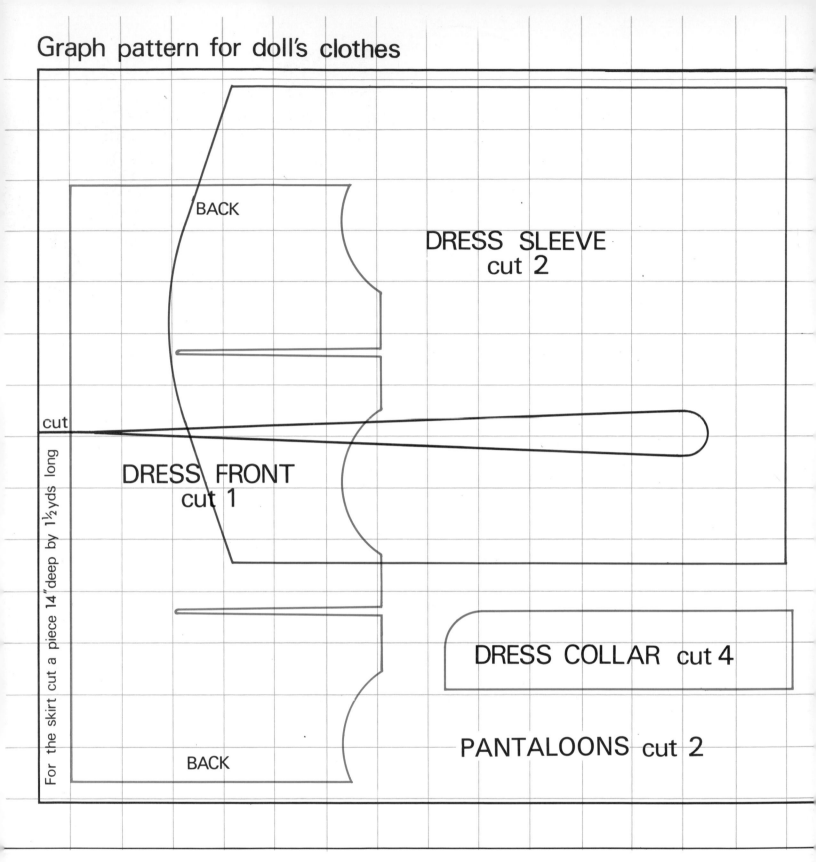

For the skirt cut a piece 14" deep by 1½yds long

cut

BACK

DRESS SLEEVE
cut 2

DRESS FRONT
cut 1

DRESS COLLAR cut 4

PANTALOONS cut 2

BACK

edges with shirring elastic 1 inch from the hem. Stitch decorative braid around the ankle hem of each leg.

Dress
Draw up the pattern pieces from the graph. Cut out the pieces from the flowered material. With right sides together, stitch the bodice shoulder seams. Turn the bodice right side out. Right sides together, stitch sleeve seams. Turn to right side and stitch a narrow double hem at the wrist edge of each

sleeve. With right sides together, stitch sleeves into armhole, drawing up the sleeve head to fit. Gather each sleeve with shirring elastic two inches from the shoulder, at the elbow, and one inch from the wrist.
With right sides together, baste and stitch the collar pieces, leaving open the lower long edge of each section. Turn to the right side and press the seam allowance of the unstitched edge. Place collar sections over the raw neck edge and stitch neatly in place.

For the dress skirt, cut a piece of flowered fabric 14 inches deep by 1½ yards long. With right sides together, stitch together the two short edges, leaving 2 inches open at one end. Press seam flat. Run a double line of gathering stitches around the upper unstitched edge and draw the skirt up to fit the bodice. Baste and stitch the skirt to the bodice. Hem the back openings and stitch on four hooks and eyes or four snap fasteners. Turn up a narrow double hem along the skirt edge.

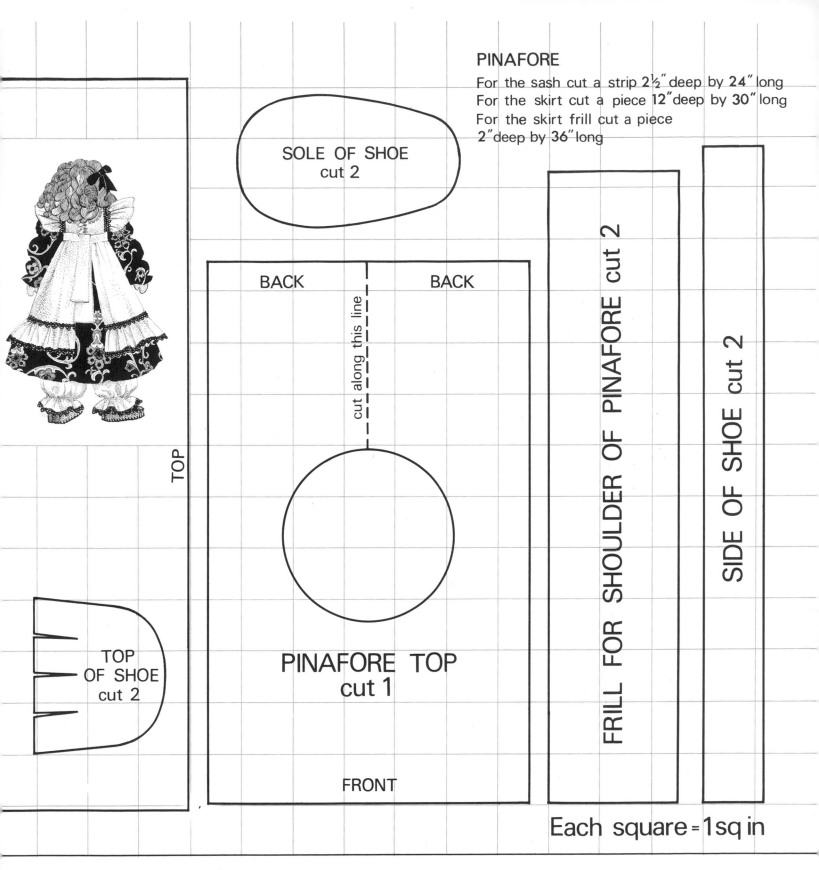

PINAFORE

For the sash cut a strip 2½" deep by 24" long
For the skirt cut a piece 12" deep by 30" long
For the skirt frill cut a piece
2" deep by 36" long

SOLE OF SHOE
cut 2

BACK   BACK

cut along this line

PINAFORE TOP
cut 1

FRONT

FRILL FOR SHOULDER OF PINAFORE cut 2

SIDE OF SHOE cut 2

TOP

TOP
OF SHOE
cut 2

Each square = 1 sq in

Pinafore

Draw up the pattern pieces from the graph and cut out the pieces from the plain fabric. From the plain fabric cut also a rectangle 12 inches deep by 2 feet 6 inches long for the pinafore skirt, a strip 2½ inches deep by 2 feet long for the sash, and a strip 2 inches deep by 3 feet long for the frill along the hem.

Turn a narrow double hem on one edge of the hem frill. Run a double row of gathering stitches along the other long edge and draw it up to fit the long edge

of the skirt section. Stitch together. Run a double line of gathering stitches along the top edge of the skirt and draw up to 12 inches. With right sides together, pin the center front of the bodice to the center front of the skirt and the center back edges of the bodice to the center back edges of the skirt. Baste and stitch. Turn a narrow double hem on the back openings, neck edge and armholes. Turn a narrow double hem on one long edge of the sleeve frills. Gather the long raw edge of each frill and draw up

and fit the armholes. Stitch in position, right side of frill to wrong side of bodice. Fold the sash strip in half lengthwise and stitch, leaving one short side open. Turn to right side and slip stitch opening. Top-stitch sash to pinafore. Work a row of cross-stitch around the neck edge of the bodice and across the front of the sash as shown in the picture. Stitch braid around skirt frill and over shoulders. Sew two buttons on one edge of the bodice back and make two corresponding loops on the opposite side.

2087

Creating an heirloom

A christening robe offers a wide choice of decorative possibilities. Choose a variety of embroidery stitches and techniques – for example, satin stitch, French knots, eyelet embroidery or shadow work – to achieve a delicate and pretty effect. Remember, however, that incorporating too many elements in one garment can create an over-complicated, fussy look.

Bits and pieces

The christening robe shown in the photograph combines both old and new features. Unbleached sheer cotton and pieces of old lace and tulle complement each other in an irresistible, creamy garment that has a charming Victorian appearance.

The embroidery on tulle used for the insertions on both christening robe and bonnet has not been worked specifically

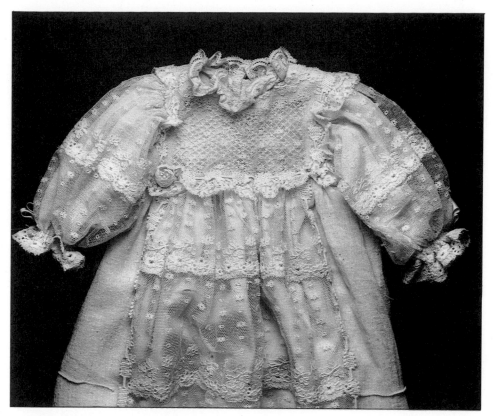

▲ Detail of the bodice reveals embroidery on net combined with machine-made lace
▼ The bonnet is trimmed with ribbon and lace edging

for this garment, but was chosen from among oddments for its suitability of style and color. This type of project is ideal for using up remnants and scraps of lace, edgings and trim, as many small oddments can be combined to make the whole.

Fine tucking is worked by machine on this christening robe across the skirt. One half-inch of material has been allowed for each quarter-inch tuck.

Other ideas

An alternative style is suggested for a christening robe of embroidered tulle. A tracing pattern is given for the embroidery motif.

Inspiration for stitchery ideas and motifs suitable for a christening robe may be taken from books, magazines and articles of hand-worked embroidery – very often adaptations and composite pieces prove to be the most successful.

Variations on the christening robe include an optional front panel, a frill or lace-trimmed yoke, tucks and any combination of embroidery stitches

sleeve

yoke

bonnet

▲ *Suggested placement of motifs*
▼ *Some decorative applications of this type of embroidery*

▲ *Tracing pattern for a piece of embroidery on net*
▼ *Close-up detail of embroidery on net*